Educational Economics
Where Do $chool Funds Go?

Also of interest from the Urban Institute Press:

Saving America's High Schools, edited by Becky A. Smerdon and Kathryn M. Borman

Good Schools in Poor Neighborhoods: Defying Demographics, Achieving Success, by Beatriz Chu Clewell and Patricia B. Campbell with Lesley Perlman

Examining Comprehensive School Reform, edited by Daniel K. Aladjem and Kathryn M. Borman

THE URBAN INSTITUTE PRESS
WASHINGTON, DC

Educational Economics

Where Do $chool Funds Go?

Marguerite Roza

THE URBAN INSTITUTE PRESS
2100 M Street, N.W.
Washington, D.C. 20037

Library of Congress Cataloging-in-Publication Data

Roza, Marguerite.
   Educational economics : where do school funds go? / Marguerite Roza.
      p. cm.
   Includes bibliographical references and index.
   ISBN 978-0-87766-764-3 (alk. paper)
   1. Education—United States—Finance. 2. Educational equalization—United States.
I. Title.
   LB2825.R67 2010
   371.2'060973--dc22

                              2009053280

Printed in the United States of America

THE URBAN INSTITUTE is a nonprofit, nonpartisan policy research and educational organization established in Washington, D.C., in 1968. Its staff investigates the social, economic, and governance problems confronting the nation and evaluates the public and private means to alleviate them. The Institute disseminates its research findings through publications, its web site, the media, seminars, and forums.

Through work that ranges from broad conceptual studies to administrative and technical assistance, Institute researchers contribute to the stock of knowledge available to guide decisionmaking in the public interest.

Conclusions or opinions expressed in Institute publications are those of the authors and do not necessarily reflect the views of officers or trustees of the Institute, advisory groups, or any organizations that provide financial support to the Institute.

Contents

     Elements of a Coherent, Aligned,
     Efficient Education Finance System   89

     Notes   101

     References   105

     About the Author   111

     Index   113

Acknowledgments

This work was funded in part by the Annie E. Casey Foundation, the Bill & Melinda Gates Foundation, and the Broad Foundation. The author would like to thank the foundations for their support but acknowledge that the findings and conclusions contained here are those of the author alone and do not necessarily reflect the opinions of the foundations.

This book was written at the encouragement of Bruno Manno, who recognized that the many discrete research studies together would create a useful whole. The author also thanks Paul Hill for a decade of encouragement in taking on education finance research. In addition, thanks go to Sanjay Bhatt, Ellen Podgorski, and Cristina Sepe for their help on individual chapters and revisions.

Introduction

E ducation finance has long been a topic of public debate. With education consuming an increasing share of public resources and adequacy cases calling for even more jumps in spending, the public is increasingly interested in how education resources are used. And the economic downturns will prompt many more questions as the public sector reconsiders spending priorities in the context of tightening budgets.

Questions about spending arise in part out of frustration with the weak link between spending and student outcomes. K–12 education spending has ballooned over the past few decades. In current dollars, U.S. taxpayers now spend almost $9,000 per pupil, which, after adjusting for inflation, still represents roughly double what was spent on each student 30 years ago. And yet, most would agree that schools are producing at best only slightly better results than three decades ago. A 30-year look at National Assessment of Educational Progress results for 17-year-olds, for instance, suggests that test scores have changed very little. Math and reading have nudged up while science and writing have dropped. How can such an infusion of funds have produced so few gains?

New research illustrates stark realities—some counterintuitive, many counterproductive—about how education resources are ultimately deployed in schools. Insights from the school level do a lot to explain the weak link between spending and student outcomes. Yet, most policy analyses consider education finance from the top down—

focusing primarily on federal and state funding priorities, policies, and legal claims.

When the federal government and states allocate funds to districts, these funds are combined with other local revenues and separated into broad categories like "instruction," "pupil support," and "administration." This raw accounting helps explain where the funds originate and how evenly (or unevenly) funds are distributed among districts.

But this accounting is just fuzzy math from the school perspective. Instead of considering the source and flow of funds, this book approaches the question by asking these four questions:

- *Who* decides to use the money this way?
- *Why* is money used this way and not some other way?
- *What* strategy drives spending decisions, and how does it relate to what the United States is trying to do for students?
- *How* do costs compare across different priorities, strategies, and objectives?

Unfortunately, existing school finance texts cannot answer these questions. Neither can the people running the system. The system is simply not set up to track the fiscal data needed to answer these types of questions. The end result is predictable: education systems flying in the dark, without meaningful baseline data on school-level spending patterns to check against academic "flight plans" or to inform mid-course corrections and adjustments to spending priorities.

For the past decade, a team of researchers at the Center on Reinventing Public Education at the University of Washington has been digging deep into school spending and uncovering elusive spending patterns in schools all over the country. The group began by asking what it thought were simple questions: How much does the district spend on each school it operates? How do spending disparities compare with district priorities? How does spending compare across student groups? After consulting many districts, the researchers are now no longer surprised that their questions are not easily answered. They are now accustomed to getting answers only by starting at the school level and building up the expenditure patterns by tracing every dollar districts spend.

The results of the Center's work and other similar analyses are startling. They point to numerous unintelligible spending patterns within and among schools and suggest that district leaders are largely unaware of where their dollars are going. In this environment, even proven education reforms may be undermined by fiscal practices, unbeknownst to district leaders. It is no surprise that increases in education spending do so little to improve student outcomes.

This book strives to explain education finance from the *school* vantage point, showing how the various funding flows inhibit or retard a school's effort to deliver services to students aligned with its academic priorities. In truth, education finance includes a host of decisions, practices, and behaviors operating at multiple stages in education bureaucracies that are instrumental in driving both the types and quantities of resources to schools. This research has meticulously tracked these disparate elements involved in determining what is purchased and how resources are used across schools.

The information assembled is never reported in school district budgets, but it is critical in understanding how the finance system truly works to bring resources to schools. The examples and data will be surprising, if not shocking, to most readers. Yet, in presenting this work elsewhere, the Center found the explanations clearly ring true with most audiences. Since almost everyone has logged countless hours in schools—first as students, later as parents—they all intuitively recognize most of the forces at play.

This work details how individuals at all levels of the system (from the federal government down to the service providers) play different roles in determining how resources are used across schools. Many players have no official budgeting capacity, nor do they recognize their roles in resource allocation. The players have different agendas, often competing, that intertwine to provide what hardly look like coherent or intentional school spending patterns.

The implications of this system on school spending patterns are also clear. How are schools spending their money? Does it go to where parents, administrators, and researchers think it goes, and is it used for what they think it's used for? The answer is often no. But perhaps more troubling, it is clear that schools are not tracking this fiscal information in ways that can answer those questions. This means decisionmakers cannot possibly use resources strategically, since they are operating in the dark.

This book describes the system as is, illustrating how the current state of affairs creates an arrangement with no accountability for resource allocation decisions, and how the competing theories of action create incoherence for schools. School spending, whether adequate or not, is anything but efficient, and there is simply no way to pinpoint those responsible for the sum of parts in place today.

As the book concludes, the finance system problems are so inherent that reconnecting spending with student outcomes will require a complete overhaul. Toward this end, the book's concluding chapter offers up a framework for an aligned, coherent finance system, one with clear roles and built-in mechanisms to promote improvements in spending productivity.

1

Fuzzy Math

Imagine a high school that spends $328 per student for math courses and $1,348 per cheerleader for cheerleading activities. Cheerleading, not math, is apparently far more important to the school, which spends four times more money per cheerleader teaching cheers than teaching math.

But this school is not imaginary. It's a real high school in a real district. And it is not even a school in a district that prioritizes cheerleading. The display cases are not filled with cheerleading awards, and the cheerleading team is no different from a typical high school cheerleading team. In fact, this district's "strategic plan" has for the past three years claimed that *math* was the primary focus. District leaders have repeatedly touted their commitment to math in response to persistently low math test scores and the local industry's calls for graduates with better math skills. What is more, students at this high school who do not pass the state's exams in math and other core subjects will not be awarded diplomas. Yet when it comes to spending public funds, this high school implicitly prioritizes cheerleading over math.

In a different school—this one in a higher-spending urban district in the eastern United States with many large high schools—the average per student cost of offering ceramics was $1,608; cosmetology, $1,997. In contrast, the cost per core subject, such as science or literary arts, was less than half that, at $739 per pupil (Roza 2009).

You may think these schools are anomalies. Most public high schools would not yield the same patterns, right? On the contrary. In the many different schools where Center on Reinventing Public Education (CRPE) researchers dug up the numbers, they regularly found a much greater per pupil investment in sports and electives than in core subjects.

How is it possible that a school can spend more money per pupil on non-core courses? In the schools studied, higher salaried (i.e., more senior) teachers often teach electives and sports—courses that typically have lower student-to-teacher ratios. In some places, labor contracts dictate that athletic coaches receive stipends. Lower student-to-teacher ratios and higher salaries of these veteran teachers drive up the costs of offering sports and electives.

After pulling together the information needed to complete these calculations, it is easy to see how each factor affects the costs. In most high schools, courses (and many sports) are given equal treatment on the daily schedule. Each course meets for an equal amount of time, say 50 minutes, five days a week. If a teacher teaches five classes in a day and each class has 30 students in it, the cost per student per course is a fairly simple division problem. Then, when you bring in the factors of real salaries, lower student-to-teacher ratios in non-core classes, and stipends for athletic coaches, the discrepancies start to appear.

After an analysis of several schools in one district showed such high costs for offering ceramics and photography courses and sports activities, CRPE obtained costs for participation in similar programs offered through the schools' adjacent community centers. The fee for enrollment in similar community center programs was always less than what the schools were paying to offer those programs to its students. Costs for ceramics, photography, some music classes, track programs, golf teams, middle and elementary basketball, and so on were all much lower than what it cost the school to offer these options. Sometimes the community center programs cost less than 10 percent of what the school was paying.

As consultants for the district, CRPE proposed that the school might pay the fees for their students to take some electives and sports through the community center. The district acknowledged that the proposal made sense, but it could not follow through because the funding used for these programs was earmarked in a voter-approved levy, which dictated that the money be used for sports and arts programs in the schools. In *who defines "sensible"*

short, the district could not let the school make a more sensible choice because of strings attached to its funding.

Who is at fault here? While we normally think of district leaders as responsible for decisions about how resources are used, clearly more parties are at play. Here, voters have a hand in the decisions, whether they recognize it or not.

The Truth about Spending on High-Needs Students

While it is not outlandish to hear that cheerleading gets more support per participant than math, most policymakers take it for granted that high-poverty schools receive more support than low-poverty schools. The link between poverty and low test scores is well documented. In response, federal and state policy have directed more resources to students from poor families, and districts have adopted similar initiatives to raise the achievement of low-performing students. But here again, the rhetoric of giving poor students a helping hand rings false when examining actual spending patterns.

Most people would agree that the teacher is perhaps the critical factor in a child's learning. So it would make sense to worry about how teacher costs differ across high- and low-poverty schools within each district. Here is what the dollar comparisons reveal: *Inside nearly every urban school district in the country, teachers are paid more to teach middle- or upper-class students than to teach high-poverty students.*

Analysis of Austin, Baltimore, Dallas, Denver, Cincinnati, Houston, Seattle, and many other school districts unequivocally shows that teacher salaries are an average of $1,000 to $5,000 higher in schools with fewer poor students than in the highest-poverty schools in the same district. In a 2002 analysis of Baltimore City, teachers at one high-poverty school were paid an average of $37,618, compared with over $57,000 at another school *in the same district*—a difference of close to $20,000 (Roza and Hill 2004). Other larger studies revealed similar salary patterns across districts in California, New York, and Texas (Education Trust—West 2005).

After collecting revenues from all taxpayers, how can districts justify paying higher salaries to teachers in some schools than in others? Here again, the explanation is fairly intuitive. All teachers in a district are paid from the same salary schedule, which provides step increases for each year of teaching experience and for taking continuing education courses or earning master's degrees. Under union contracts or historical arrangements, teachers with even one or two years of experience have some say over where they teach, and many teachers choose to avoid the most challenging schools. When one school has very senior teachers with master's degrees and another school is staffed primarily with rookies, therein lie the differences in average teacher salaries across the schools.

Generally speaking, district budgets that break down spending by school do not display these differences. Here is why: Any given school in a district has an average teacher salary used for accounting and the *real* average teacher salary. The former does not vary from school to school because it is the mathematical average salary for all teachers in the district. The latter, however, varies tremendously from school to school because not all schools have a mix of teacher experience that mirrors the district average. In reporting publicly how much is spent in any given school, most districts use the *accounting* average teacher salary, not the real one. While that might make the number crunching more straightforward for district-level accounting staff, it hides school-level spending inequities.

These data, like the data on expenditure patterns across core and elective courses, were at first difficult to obtain. When CRPE started asking about real teacher salaries, district fiscal staff said that those were in completely different databases, and if CRPE wanted those, it would need to call the personnel department. When CRPE investigated further, it found the same pattern in district after district.

District fiscal staff defend the practice of creating school budgets with the districtwide average teacher salary. In theory, this policy ensures that, all costs being equal, high-poverty schools can compete with low-poverty schools for the most experienced, educated, and expensive teachers. If school budgets were developed based on real salaries, the theory goes, high-poverty schools would not be able to afford the most expensive teachers, or they would be forced to raise class sizes to hire the few they could afford.

The truth is the highest-salaried teachers tend to avoid high-poverty schools and concentrate at schools that serve predominantly middle- and upper-class students. Schools in wealthier neighborhoods often receive over a hundred applications for a teacher vacancy, while schools in poor neighborhoods might receive only two or three (Roza 2007d). On average, given that each school can hire the best talent available, schools with more applicants get more talent. And, schools with the most applicants actually employ higher salaried teachers.[1] Schools with much smaller applicant pools have fewer hiring choices and end up with lower-salaried teachers; they then have a difficult time retaining teachers to create a stable teacher corps.

In short, the real average salary for all teachers at a given school reflects the school's ability to hire teachers and can thus indicate teacher quality. There is good reason to believe that schools with higher overall salaries have their pick of much larger applicant pools and likely end up with more capable teachers, lower teacher turnover, more stable workforces, and other critical differences that matter for student learning.

Why do all districts not track and report to the public the real average salary for all teachers in every school? District leaders, of course, would be confronted with public shock and dismay over the gap in spending on teacher salaries between high-poverty and low-poverty schools. But they also might have to admit a more perverse effect of their accounting rules: the transfer of public funds from poorer to wealthier schools in the district.

The only way districts can afford to pay the pricier teachers that congregate in more advantaged schools is by drawing on the dollars saved on the cheaper teachers in the high-poverty schools. It is a zero-sum game. In a game where budgets are based on the districtwide average salary, affluent schools get a bargain on their pricey veteran teachers, while high-poverty schools pay a premium for their low-cost novice teachers.

Districts have not followed through on overcoming the effects of poverty by trying to invest more in high-needs students. Certainly, some targeted allocations (described more in later chapters) layer on these lopsided allocations to bring more programs or services to the high-needs schools. Yet given the uneven distribution of teacher costs, these special programs only put a bandage on the problem. The fundamental problem is an outmoded array of resource allocation policies—particularly, the fixed salary schedule, the way teachers are assigned to schools, and the use of districtwide average teacher salaries in school budgets. These policies all work together to drive more public dollars to higher-performing kids. Again, the implicit strategy at hand contradicts what education leaders promote explicitly.

These conflicting data have been available for some time. Many district leaders now seem to understand how their resource allocation policies actually shortchange high-needs schools. Yet all but just a few districts in the country continue to operate this way. Districts lack the political will to change policies established decades ago for a factory-model school system. Powerful forces work to protect the interests of those who benefit from the present allocation of resources. Among those who benefit from the status quo are the more experienced teachers, influential parents with children in high-achieving schools, and board members who represent wealthier neighborhoods.

Understanding the Weak Link between Spending and Student Outcomes

For decades, researchers have struggled to define the link between money and student outcomes. Beginning with the Coleman report in 1966, research has questioned basic assumptions about how resources affect student outcomes. Since then, the literature on the relationship between resources and outcomes has been mixed. Some researchers argue that money may positively influence student achievement if it is used in concert with specific reforms (Murnane and Levy 1996). Others argue that additional money is more important for minority or disadvantaged students (Duncombe and Yinger 2004; Rothstein 2004). Yet, some studies show that increasing funds to schools has not significantly raised student test scores (Nyhan and Alkadry 1999). Despite the claims these studies make about outcomes and funding, they provide little evidence about why the system either succeeds or fails to relate money to student achievement.

Findings from traditional production function studies that the effects of resources are, more often than not, statistically insignificant are often interpreted as "money doesn't make a difference." This interpretation reflects the relatively small and variable effects of school resources versus the powerful and consistent effects of family background. These debates generally revolve around technical issues of model specification, sampling, and data analysis.

So, while the research continues to focus on aggregated finance databases, the answer to the problem of why funds are poorly linked to student outcomes lies more in how funds are realized at the school level. That is where the rubber meets the road, and where and how resources are deployed across students defines the relationship between funds and outcomes. In other words, tightening the link between spending and outcomes requires understanding the finance system from the school vantage point.

Botched Reform Attempts amid Too Many Cooks

The No Child Left Behind (NCLB) Act and other accountability reforms undoubtedly put pressure on districts to raise test scores in their lowest-performing schools. Most districts now have some strategy for raising test scores in their lowest-performing schools. The problem is, districts have not taken stock of these strategies to see if they raise spending at the high-needs schools to levels above the spending at lower-needs schools.

In a study of the four biggest districts in Texas and the Denver public schools, in all but Dallas, a greater level of flexible base funding (defined as state and local funds not targeted to specific student types) went to the wealthiest quartile of schools—at least 10 percent more in each district (Roza, Miller, and Hill 2005).[2] Some, but not all, of the difference came from salaries. In each case (except Dallas), the district allocated more staff to the wealthier schools, which also drove up costs. Ignoring the effect of salary differences, the added staff positions resulted in up to 12 percent more spending on schools in the wealthiest quartile.

Amid efforts to target resources to high-needs students, how does practice demonstrate the opposite? Because of a multitude of allocation practices that ultimately do not add up to the intended result. First, those extra allocations that benefit the less needy schools: these allocations might be an expanded music program in one school, extra technology staff in another, specialists to support a magnet program, or an art history pilot in a subset of schools. Sometimes these programs are earmarked with funds by state lawmakers or are pet projects of district central office departments. Some are the result of local levy prescriptions or are the by-products of teacher labor contract negotiations. Still others simply land on certain schools with powerful principals or are bargains struck with powerful parent groups. In most cases, the flow of dollars helps show how many different players have their hands in resource allocation.

So, while districts have added new programs and services for high-needs students, these new programs layer on to an already-messy allocation system, much of which benefits the less needy schools. With so many cooks involved, the results are incoherent, misaligned, and often inefficient allocations that can fly in the face of districts' intentions to focus more programs and services on the most needy schools. The truth is, districts have not taken stock of all their programs to see if the new programs, services, and efforts have overridden the many extras that wealthier schools receive.

In fact, urban legends say that the opposite problem exists: recent spending decisions are investing so much in remedial services that high achievers are getting shortchanged. A recent study by the Thomas B. Fordham Institute finds that teachers believe high-performing students receive less attention that do average or struggling students (Loveless, Farkas, and Duffett 2008).

Yet, according to data from several high schools, this is not the case. In one district, remedial courses cost $712 per pupil, whereas the district spends $1,400 to $1,600 per advanced placement (AP) or honors course. In another district, the honors classes cost between 25 and 80 percent more than the remedial courses (Roza 2009).

A lot of cost factors are involved in these examples, many of which are not under the control of the school and some of which are not under control of the district. Remedial classes are taught in larger student groups by lower-salaried teachers, and the teachers teach more classes per day (five versus four). In addition, labor contract provisions control the daily schedule, class length, and salary schedules. In one example, the state sets class size limits for AP classes but not remedial classes; this limit also plays a role in the discrepancies.

These spending patterns go largely unrecognized, even though the implicit strategies of those patterns directly conflict with districts' stated priorities. Education leaders simply do not know whether their investments support their stated objectives because their districts do not collect and report costs per course per pupil.

Then, even those allocations intended for low performers do not actually bring more funds to the intended groups. In one state with persistently low science scores, the state legislature stepped in—as state legislatures often do on educational resource decisions—and determined that each school in the state would receive a "science coach" to help teachers incorporate more science in their curriculum. But again, the dollar value of such an investment was not computed and assessed for its distribution across the state's different schools. When the costs of a science coach are divided across different-sized schools, the per pupil investment of such a plan varies dramatically by school.

The result: In a state where the largest schools are the neediest, this investment disproportionately brought more resources per pupil to less needy schools. In a state where science performance was higher in the small schools, the investment effectively widened the gap by focusing more dollars on the smaller schools.

Infusing Transparency, Alignment, and Coherence into Education Spending

If one subscribes to the textbook explanation that an organization's resource allocation system is a manifestation of its strategic priorities, then here is what CRPE research has shown is most important to urban districts throughout the nation: Middle- and upper-class students, not poor students. Electives and athletics, not core subjects. Gifted and high-achieving students, not struggling students. With implicit priorities like these playing out at the school level, it is no surprise that the system produces such a weak link between spending and goals for student outcomes.

How can those inside and outside the system allow such blatantly contradictory spending patterns to persist in their own schools? They generally do not know these patterns exist, as district budgeting and accounting practices make it incredibly difficult to identify detailed spending patterns. Frankly, the five-inch-thick binders of impenetrable financial information plunked down in front of school board members do not even include this essential information.

How did this happen, and who is to blame? Clearly, there is no one locus of control for education spending. Legally, school board members are assigned responsibility for resource use, but as the examples here indicate, education is also partly governed by the federal and state governments and the voting public. Funds come in the district door with numerous conditions and prescriptions for their use. Once inside the district, the funds are subject to the influence of numerous stakeholders before they are brought to bear on students. Layer on the historical arrangements, and the result is a spending picture that is anything but what is stated in most districts' strategy documents.

Once those in key leadership positions and the larger public understand how funds are not being invested in step with their priorities, one hopes they will demand the wholesale change needed to tackle this dysfunctional system. If Americans believe that implicit financial strategies are critical to the success of stated objectives for students, then changing the system becomes a national imperative. Part of the challenge will be to help the different layers in the system recognize their own roles in dictating spending patterns. Once they throw out the fuzzy math, education leaders may find their decisions can add up to something real.

2

Who's in Charge Here?

One is likely to think of budgeting as an arid subject, the province of stodgy clerks and dull statisticians. Nothing could be more mistaken.
—Aaron Wildavsky (from Wildavsky and Caiden 2004)

The way Americans finance K–12 public education should be a topic of broad interest if for nothing more than that it accounts for the biggest slice of state and local government budgets. All told, the public spends some $500 billion annually on K–12 public education, or an average of $8,701 per pupil. This national average, however, is a crude measure of spending because K–12 public education in the United States is intensely localized. Per pupil spending ranges from $5,500 in Utah to more than $14,000 in New York (National Education Association 2005), yet those averages, too, disguise vast spending disparities among districts and even schools.

These huge ranges at each level—state, district, and school—obfuscate discussions on national education policy. In other words, almost any assertion on spending patterns that may be true at, say, the national or state level is meaningless or, worse, inaccurate at the school level.

This dissonance and its consequences are not widely understood by the public, nor are reforms analyzed from the context of the school level. But the school-level view of allocating resources is critical to any serious efforts to give an equitable, quality education to all students. The vantage point from the school presents an entirely different perspective on how America finances public education, one that most books on education finance policy do not deal with directly.

Most literature on education finance issues discusses finances from the top-down view of federal and state policymakers. For those new to the topic, this chapter reviews some larger trends in education finance that will serve as a foundation for the discussion in later chapters on the deficiencies of the current system. The chapter also explores some often-overlooked forces that influence allocation decisions within a school district. The picture that emerges is of a fragmented school finance system pulled in separate directions, lacking consistency and coherence, with little chance of being able to right itself.

Where the Money Originates

The primary responsibility for funding public education today rests with the states—which account for nearly 50 percent of the nation's spending on K–12 public education—and local school districts, which account for another 44 percent of total spending. Though the federal government is a minor player in total K–12 public spending, contributing less than 10 percent, it has dramatically influenced the finance policies of state and local education agencies through federal mandates, congressional earmarks, and judicial oversight.

Starting in the early 1970s, state and U.S. Supreme Court rulings established that basic education funding is primarily a state responsibility. Previously, basic education funding was considered mainly the purview of local government. The *Serrano v. Priest* case (1971) in California is regarded as the first in a series of modern-era school funding lawsuits filed on behalf of individuals in property-poor districts who argued successfully that their schools were unable to provide as good an education as those in property-rich districts.[1] By notching a victory in California, public-interest attorneys established a model for litigation against other states' school funding systems, a strategic direction later forced by the U.S. Supreme Court's 1973 ruling in *San Antonio Independent School District v. Rodriguez* that education was not a fundamental right under the Constitution.[2]

While the details of state funding systems vary substantially, nearly all use some basic education funding mechanism driven by student enrollment and augment that with other funds for specific services or initiatives, such as special education or reduced class size. The Education Commission of the States recently published a report that found that most states were using one of three approaches in 2002 for allocating basic education resources (Griffith 2008). Half of states (including Florida, Texas, and Colorado) and the District of Columbia provided "foundation" funding—that is, a minimum base allocation, weighted by type of student (for example, English language learner)—to each district. A dozen other states, including California, New York, and Michigan, used a modified foundation formula in which the base amount provided by the state varies from district to district. Seven states (including North Carolina, Tennessee, Delaware, and Washington) allocated funds to districts for educational staff, such as teachers and administrators, based on total student enrollment. State funding formulas are perennially scrutinized by education reformers, and lawsuits to invalidate education funding systems in several states make for a dynamic policy landscape.

Both state and federal agencies supplement the basic education funds with restricted funds, known as categorical grants, which the recipients are required to spend on specific types of students or services. Some of these grants come to schools and districts indirectly from federal agencies, while others flow directly from the revenue source, typically the state or local education district. These revenue streams come with strict rules about how the grants are to be administered, what can be purchased, and how resources can be distributed and the funds then accounted for.

It is only in reading the fine print of each state's funding formulas that the differences in allocations for different student types emerge. For example, targeted allocations may take the form of per student allocations, flat grants, competitive grants, staff allocations, funds for specific services, reimbursements of costs, cost sharing, and limited eligibility grants (often funding only those with high concentrations of a specific student type). A key difference is whether the state allocation works primarily to increase spending in the district, restricts the use of funds so they only benefit a certain student type, or specifies exactly what program or service is provided with the funds. Also relevant, formulas can include enrollment of a particular student demographic, the concentration of that subpopulation, local effort in funding education, and previous years' allocations (Carey 2002).

In sifting through federal and state allocations that target resources to different student types, one can immediately see how allocation formula details help determine ultimate spending levels across districts and schools. Targeted allocations differ enormously, with some allocating

---

Box 2.1. Sample Allocation Details

Types of Targeted Allocations
- Lump-sum grants
- Per pupil
- Per fixed (or capped) percentage of all pupils
- Per school
- Per staff (allocations for training)
- Programs or services (e.g., professional development, reduced class size)
- Staff (e.g., instructional aides, coaches)
- Expenditure reimbursements

Types of Restrictions
- Which schools are eligible
- Which students are eligible
- What objects can be purchased (and at what amounts)
- What services are covered
- How nongrant dollars are expended (i.e., requires match, comparability, non-supplanting, etc.)
- Separate accounting

---

dollars and others allocating staff or programs. Box 2.1 shows some of the ways allocations are made.

The most notable federal categorical grant is the Title I program. Now more than 40 years old and currently allocated as part of No Child Left Behind, this program allocates over $13 billion to districts serving high concentrations of children from low-income families. In total, approximately 41 percent of all federal K–12 education dollars are allocated to programs for economically disadvantaged children. Other examples of categorical federal funding programs are those for students with disabilities, vocational education, and bilingual education.

All the different funding streams then collide at the district level. Local districts are generally responsible for converting all their apportioned funds from the state and federal government into expenditures for programs or services allocated to schools. Many formulas, practices, and forces that drive resource distribution remain undocumented, unclear, and at times mysterious to all but the budget staff. In general, the process involves a staff-based formula to allocate full-time staff to schools based on increments of student enrollment, such as a teacher for every 25 students and a vice principal when enrollment exceeds 400. Additional staff can be allocated case by case, such as a music teacher for a specific magnet school or a technology specialist in an innovative high school. Many districts then add staff to cover special programs for needier students and assign the costs to categorical funds.

A substantial portion of the district budget is allocated to central administration, and the department directors distribute these funds generally at their discretion. Costs for noneducational services, such as food, transportation, and utilities, are generally covered from the central administration's portion of the budget. The division of operating funds between central administration and schools also varies from district to district. In districts where schools have the power to decide how to allocate their budget, more than a few choose not to purchase services from the central administration and instead outsource that service or reprogram the allocation for a more urgent need. Such decentralized financial decisionmaking requires strong school accountability and flexible collective bargaining agreements, both of which tend to be the exception rather than the rule.

In summary, today's education finance system operates on revenue mainly from state and local governments, allocates resources to districts based on formula, and supplements them with restricted funds targeted at specific educational needs or priorities. This architecture is highly organic and sensitive to the demands of political currents. Over the past 30 years, four political themes have significantly influenced state and local education finance policies. Each had merits on its face but fell short in producing desired outcomes at the school level.

Attempts at Equity

Many states are preoccupied with seeking equity across *districts*. As mentioned previously in the *Serrano* case in California, inequities in funding across property-rich and property-poor school districts set in motion two decades of litigation that forced states to address spending differences among districts. The basic premise of the litigation was that discrepancies in access to resources gave some students a higher quality of public education than others, violating individuals' right to equal protection under the law. That is, the more a district spent per pupil, the better education it could deliver than a district that spent less per pupil.

As a result of the equity litigation, most states adopted an equalization mechanism that leverages state and local funds to provide more equal access to resources across districts. Some states limit what can be collected locally. Others combine state dollars with local funds to provide a foundation, or base, allocation to every district.

Yet despite the attention given to equity *across* districts in state policy, equalization efforts have done virtually nothing to address inequities *within* districts. The equalization effort in New York was prompted by reports that New York City spends an average of $4,000 less per pupil than affluent Westchester County; what goes unspoken, though, is that individual schools in New York City spend over $6,000 more per pupil than other schools in the same district (Roza and Hill 2006).

Such *intradistrict* spending inequities continue despite having nothing to do with access to revenues and more to do with district distribution policies. The district sends out teachers, principals, administrative assistants, lunch room staff, librarians, and the like, and pays the bills out of the district coffers. Schools do not have their own bank accounts, nor do they receive reports that show the true costs of the resources that land in their buildings. Districts rarely compute what they spend on each school, much less compare across schools or worry about equity. Thus, district resource-allocation practices routinely perpetuate the stark inequities that state policies were intended to minimize. These inequities are harder to quantify and report publicly because they are *intradistrict* instead of *interdistrict*.

Attempts to Subsidize Services for Some Students

Besides efforts to equalize access to resources among students, state and federal policymakers have gradually tried to wrest resource allocation authority away from local school boards by adding restrictions to the use of their categorical funds. These restrictions focus on targeting the funds to needy students and raising their achievement. The Title I program's rationale for setting aside supplemental funds for low-income students was that, on average, poverty is the strongest predictive factor in student performance.

Forty years later, poverty still is the most powerful indicator of student performance—and that sad reality supports the widespread belief that categoricals have not effectively addressed the issues they had targeted. Despite their apparent ineffectiveness, federal and state categoricals have grown in number and amount.

Policymakers have gradually restricted the spending not just to specific groups of students (such as low-income English language learners) but also to specific programs or services. These new categoricals include funding for early childhood education, tutoring in reading, smaller class sizes, small high schools, science coaches, and other interventions that reformers hope will somehow raise student achievement.

Occasionally grounded in solid research, these programs or services almost always have an aggressive political constituency determined to fight for their existence. In fact, the most recent Catalog of Federal Domestic Assistance lists 87 education programs.[3]

More recently, Congress has created *customized* categoricals in the form of earmarks. Buried in the voluminous federal appropriation bill sent to the president each year are earmarks, also known as set-asides, that fund specific projects or programs at schools or districts favored by a member of Congress's delegation. At first, only a few programs or institutions benefited, but by 2005, the U.S. Department of Education appropriations bill included hundreds of set-asides that accounted for hundreds of millions in spending.

A quick read of the list of identified recipients shows the nature and scope of the problem: A program in a Florida receives $160,000 for equipment and technology, a school district in Wisconsin receives $1,200,000 for after-school programs, a Kentucky school district receives $300,000 to support teacher excellence, and a Washington district receives $320,000 for a family literacy program.[4]

Federal set-asides circumvent all education finance mechanisms and frustrate efforts at equalizing schools' access to resources. Earmarks are granted based on political favor, not on either demonstrated needs or competition. Because of complaints, there is now a temporary moratorium on set-asides in the education budget, but new rules may allow them to resume.

States have followed the federal lead by becoming more prescriptive with new education funding, instead of simply increasing basic education funds. Wisconsin now has 34 categoricals, South Carolina has 74, and California has 124. In fact, California's special programs accounted for almost $3 billion in the 2006–07 budget, nearly 6 percent of the total education budget. This staggering amount covers everything from school nutrition programs to counselors to organic gardens.

States were able to layer on categoricals—and districts were able to administer them—partly because of the budgeting and accounting systems created in response to the federal government's categoricals. In the end, these relatively new allocations magnify the effects of the federal grants by restricting spending and fragmenting local programs even further.

To put it another way, the growth of categoricals has made it all but impossible for schools to plan programs holistically in which the parts *consistently* support a defined objective and course of action over many years. Instead, schools are forced to cobble together funded programs that may or may not be aligned with individual student needs and to replace their curricula, services, and even staff with every change in categorical programs.

Although some people recognize that the growth of categoricals produced such undesirable consequences, they have difficulty eliminating categoricals because of their entrenched constituencies. Those who benefit include the schools and districts that receive funds, and the parents and community groups that doggedly lobby for them. Categoricals also promote fiefdoms in state agencies and, often, school districts. Staff in state agencies or districts who are paid with federal funds express more loyalty to their federal administrators than to their own leadership (Cross and Roza 2007).

Attempts at Adequacy

Once equalization efforts failed and categoricals became corrupted, another policy trend began to identify how much it costs to get all students to proficiency standards in reading, writing, and math, as mandated by the federal No Child Left Behind Act.

In this more recent wave of education school finance litigation, plaintiffs are petitioning the courts to require states to allocate an "adequate" amount of funds to ensure all students achieve at least these standards. Some attempts to achieve adequate funding are massive, such as the New York ruling in 2006 that required state officials to increase the operating budget by $5,000 per student and to spend $9.2 billion on capital improvements over five years (West and Peterson 2007). In general, urban school districts are pursuing these legal actions against the state, arguing that the current funds allocated for educating the students are insufficient. Under NCLB, districts face increasingly severe sanctions if they cannot produce higher pass rates on state achievement tests than they did in the previous year. The sanctions range from forcing the district to accommodate student transfer requests to state officials taking over and operating the district.

While it is generally agreed that more money can buy a richer educational experience—compare the per pupil spending of $30,000 or more at an elite private school with the $7,000 spent per pupil at a typical public school—this view misses the importance of districts' choices about how they spend their funds.

The plaintiffs in these cases argue that if only districts had access to adequate funds, schools would have enough resources to provide an adequate education. The flaw is in assuming that spending at any given school is closely related to the district's calculation of average school spending.

For example, a 2004 Texas A&M study indicated that about $6,200 per pupil is needed to provide an adequate education for districts in Texas (Joint Select Committee on Public School Finance 2004). In Fort Worth, where the average nontargeted expenditure was $5,850 in 2003–04, the district was already spending at least this much on 17 of the district's 111 schools. In Houston, expenditures exceeded $6,200 in 121 of the district's 260 schools. In fact, at one school the district spent $9,400, while at another it spent only $3,750.

In an analysis of the Denver public schools in 2005, about a quarter of the schools received more than 110 percent of the district average expenditure. Some 30 percent received less than 90 percent of the district average (Roza et al. 2005).

While adequacy calculations differ in their approach, data, and ultimately their determinations, the examples above suggest that adequacy calculations based on existing district spending averages are inherently flawed. Nothing in the claims of adequacy plaintiffs weakens the forces within districts that lavish some schools with resources and shortchange others.

Further, determining what amount of resources is adequate depends greatly on how the resources will be used. The amount of resources necessary to deliver a particularly defined quality of education if resources are used efficiently is very different than the amount necessary if resources are distributed inefficiently. Teachers will still prefer working in low-poverty schools. The newest and least qualified teachers still will be left in the toughest schools, just as the students in those schools will be left with them. With higher-paid teachers teaching higher-performing students, one can hardly argue that the current allocation systems are efficiently closing the achievement gap.

More is already being spent on some schools than the current wave of lawsuits claims is adequate. District decisionmaking favors low-poverty schools because of their stability, the quality of leadership and teaching staff they can attract, and the activism of influential parents. The lawsuits leave the districts' decisionmaking processes intact, making it likely that additional funds will follow the same allocation patterns as existing funds.

Attempts at Efficiency

While the courts try to resolve the question of adequacy in education spending, the latest policy trend to emerge is pressuring districts to make existing funds more productive. This recent angle seems to be a response to the fact that state forecasts predict increasingly tight state budgets, leaving little new funds for education reforms, and accusations that education spending has ballooned in recent decades without corresponding gains in student performance.[5]

Efforts to get more bang for the buck can be manifested through various policy instruments, some of which work in dramatically different ways. In several states, existing legislative proposals toward getting more for the state's education dollar center on either pushing down decision-making to the school level or pulling it up to the state level. South Carolina and Delaware, for instance, are considering a new funding structure that would rescind funding prescriptions and send funds directly to schools. Different proposals floating amid California's state leadership reflect each angle: one proposes more state authority over how funds are spent, and the other proposes less. Efficiency efforts are also trying to change teacher compensation. For example, new salary incentive structures are targeted to lure teachers to some schools or reward more effective teachers, unlike more traditional salary structures that base teachers' financial compensation only on seniority and graduate credits earned.

The federal NCLB law was designed in large part to bring accountability to schools and districts in hopes that accountability would motivate school officials to focus their resources toward greater student outcomes. And, some of the sanctions for districts that fail to raise student achievement over time are based on the premise that someone else can be more productive with the same level of funds— private tutors, another public school, or a charter school, if one exists in the district.

Here again, these efforts are still relatively new and have not been fully implemented in ways that change the diffuse nature of spending decisions. The proposed solutions stop short of directly addressing some of the forces at play (some described in later sections) in the resource allocation system.

The School District Bureaucracy

The school district, while smaller, is not necessarily simpler than state education agencies. School districts vary in size across states and locales; some have a single school, while others have more than 100 schools and 100,000 students. In any case, the district is officially responsible for education resource decisions, and the district is legally accountable when funds are misused.

In most districts, leadership is officially awarded to a publicly elected school board, generally consisting of three to nine members. That means that for the 16,000 or so districts in the country, more than 100,000 local board members are officially responsible for deciding how money is used in schools. School board members, since they are publicly elected, come with varying levels of fiscal and management expertise. For most of these elected officials, this fiscal budget is the largest they have ever been responsible for, and this is their first public office. The vast majority of school board positions are unpaid. For their stewardship and countless hours of sitting through public meetings, many of them rancorous, they rarely receive public praise; little wonder that those who run for office sometimes have special interests backing them or their own pet projects or agendas.

A key responsibility of the school board is to hire the superintendent, who is at least functionally at the helm. Yet, the leadership structures are more complicated than those in many urban districts. Mayors play a more official role in district leadership in some cities. In others, state departments of education have taken over. Many states also have regional offices that provide support staff to groups of typically small school districts, creating an intermediary step between states and districts. In many school districts, the superintendent wields considerable influence over the school board, which serves as little more than a rubber stamp.

Regardless of the dynamic between the elected board and the appointed superintendent, when big money problems surface, heads nearly always roll. In the past five years, nearly half of all big-city superintendent firings have been directly or indirectly because of financial mismanagement. Baltimore, Seattle, and Oakland are all recent examples: superintendents persuaded their school boards to invest in big school improvement plans just weeks before it became evident that the district was broke and could not even keep its existing commitments.

Tracking how districts allocate resources across schools is not just a frustrating exercise for board members trying to advocate for their constituents. As mentioned previously, the forces that drive the distribution of resources to schools are unclear, frequently undocumented, and mysterious to even district staff.

For example, in one district, the psychology team consists of four psychologists, each of whom is assigned to serve all students in about 10 schools. In interviews with the psychologists about where they spend their time, one clearly spends her time in equal increments across all 10 schools. Another says she spends most of her time at a school where the principal "values her work." Another spends the largest portion of her days at the school her own child attends, and the last one focuses on the two schools he feels need his services the most. In this case, the allocation of this resource across schools depends on the psychologists' own discretion and priorities, which may or may not reflect the district's stated strategy for reform.

In another example, many districts staff each school with a librarian who is a full-time staff employee with particular skills and a job assignment. The full-time librarian is one approach to making sure reading and research materials are available to students. Other approaches might involve distributing these duties among teachers or in partnerships with public libraries. By dictating the use of the resource, the allocation asserts central authority and creates some level of uniformity across schools in how resources are used at each site.

These examples demonstrate that whether districts are aware of it or not, a host of factors affects how resources are used, controlled, targeted, and distributed to schools and students. As one research study shows, central department funds are converted into many different forms before being deployed to schools (Roza 2007a). The findings, reflected in figure 2.1, demonstrate the range of these forms in one urban district. In this district, a larger share of resources is deployed in staff assigned to schools, program access, and roaming specialists than in flexible funds, professional development, or other resources. What the research cannot yet tell is how these different forms of resources matter for schools. Per-

Figure 2.1. How Central Funds Are Allocated in One Urban School District

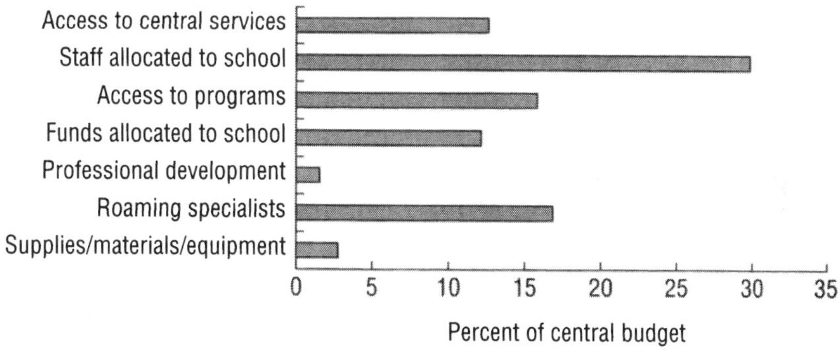

Source: Author's calculations based on Roza (2007a).

haps more important, districts do not have a sense of what they are providing and how those resources fit with the overall district strategy for reform.

In tracking the allocations in these and other districts, CRPE research has also discovered that an uncomfortable share of district resources flows out in ways that cannot be described neatly in fiscal reports but that explain the haphazardness of the findings that emerge when studying actual spending. For instance, the chief financial officer in one district spoke of how the athletic director nagged daily until he received an 8 percent increase in the athletic budget during a time of declining revenues. In another district, the professional development director made a presentation directly to the school board to explain why more investment in training was needed. The budget director in another district told us how the superintendent promised the special education director an air-conditioning unit for her office in a deal to keep her from leaving the district.

Based on these anecdotes, the CRPE team further investigated allocations to better understand what practices were in place that drove the allocations out to the different schools. In two districts studied, a little more than half all allocations followed a range of different formulas. The formulas varied in their mechanics, with some driven by enrollment, student type, school, staff counts, and so on.

The remainder of the allocations—the nearly half that were non-formulaic—were much more elusive. Data from figure 2.2 illustrate what

Figure 2.2. How Nonformulaic Allocations Are Distributed in One Urban School District

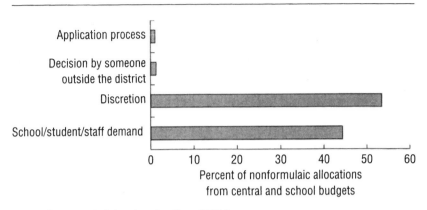

Source: Author's calculations based on Roza (2007a).

CRPE found when trying to code how or why nonformulaic allocations were deployed in the way they were ultimately realized on schools.

As the figure demonstrates, most nonformulaic allocations were driven out by the discretion of a central office staff member (53 percent). When discretion is the primary driver for an allocation, an individual in the school system uses his discretion to decide how resources are distributed among schools. For example, the athletic director mentioned above described how he used his discretion to decide where to direct new funds awarded in the study year. In this case, he decided to hire two additional assistant coaches for each of the three largest high schools and ordered all new equipment for the two middle schools with the highest percentages of athletes. He could have just as easily made different decisions, say, deploying those funds more evenly among students at each level or targeting resources to schools where students were not participating in sports to boost involvement in athletics. Similarly, the psychologist in the prior example used her discretion to decide in which schools to spend her time, and again discretion drove the resources out.

The second-largest practice for deploying resources was by demand (44 percent). Demand-driven allocations suggest that the resources flow to a school, teacher, or student only when they are requested by the end user. For instance, one district's centrally managed allocations provided music lessons for students who signed up for them. In another example, an art history program involved placing a full-time art expert in two schools in a district. When asked how the schools were selected, a central administrator said that the program was offered to two schools where the principal exhibited the most interest in the program. For an optional professional development training session, these resources were brought those teachers who opted to attend.

While these micro-level decisions have serious consequences for how resources are allocated, in many cases district leaders accept them without thought or careful examination. As would be expected, these two allocation types—discretion and demand—yield highly erratic and inconsistent spending patterns, even differing from year to year. Also, many district staff members were unaware of their role in subjective allocation decisions, and they did not realize that resources could have been deployed differently. Staff often talked about "how things are done here," and, when probed, seemed not to realize that the practices represented choices or decisions by the staff involved.

For example, the psychologists who were directed to serve 10 schools yet chose to narrow their efforts to just one or two schools did not seem to recognize their own time as a resource over which they had any control. When asked about it, one psychologist in this district responded:

> I'm a school psychologist. I just cover the schools in my assignment area. I go where the need is because that's what I'm supposed to do. I have no input into district resource decisions. Those decisions are all done by senior leadership. I don't get my own supply budget or anything. If I want the district to fund something, I need to file a purchase order request and who knows if that would get approved. (Roza 2007a)

Other Influential Forces in Resource Allocation

Labor unions also influence how resources get used within a district. Education is a labor-intensive business; a large portion of the district's operating expenses goes directly to paying and supporting the millions of school employees, and teacher contracts play a big role in determining where such resources are deployed. Through collective bargaining, labor unions can influence not just the level of salaries, but also how salaries are structured, school calendars, class size limits, the use of aides, professional development, and many other aspects of the education system.

Voters also dictate the use of resources within districts, which go to the electorate regularly for approval of operating and capital levies. Once in a while voters also weigh in on an education-related referendum, usually one with statewide scope, such as class size reduction, pre-K funding, or charter school authorization.

While unions and voters steer most of a district's budget in a particular direction, private foundations often influence spending with highly targeted matching grants. These grants act like categoricals, restricting their use for particular programs of interest to the benefactor, and also like venture capital, testing a new program for a limited time. Though big names like the Bill and Melinda Gates Foundation have made headlines for their impact on redesigning high schools in urban districts, many smaller foundations operate behind the scenes as well, some taking an active investment-like approach toward grantees and others a more passive approach based on requests received from the community.

Parents and community members influence spending in both organized and unorganized ways. Parents band to block school closures and prevent budget cuts to cherished programs. In one district, students marched into a board meeting playing their musical instruments, thus saving the middle-school music program in a single school. In another district, individual parents concerned with levels of lead found in school drinking fountains brought bottles of dirty water to board meetings and enticed local media into carrying sensational stories about autistic children who may have been exposed to the dirty water. Though no coalition ever formed, the negative publicity pushed the school board to reallocate a significant portion of its capital budget toward water quality, resulting in the cancellation of at least one school construction project.

As the examples above show, individual players within and outside the system have a powerful impact on resource allocation. More than the influence of any other factor, schools that receive more than their share of funds are simply better at working the system, despite formulas intended to create equitable access to resources.

This opportunistic behavior is the most consistent driver of unintended variations in spending across schools. There are principals who know how to get the best teachers, and those who skate through budget cuts. There are vice principals who can get the most from the three psychologists working in the central office. There are parent-teacher clubs that make sure that the grant-funded specialist stays on the district budget when the grant ends. And there are school board members that manipulate formulas to tip the balance to their schools.

If it sounds like a cutthroat competition for resources, it is. It is a competition that rewards schools based on political connections and popularity, not demonstrated needs or alignment with district goals for closing the achievement gap. If the push for accountability is to get any traction, resource allocation decisions—whether inside or outside districts—will have to become more transparent, coherent, and aligned with the districts' stated strategies for improving student achievement.

The next chapter illustrates how the system described here works at cross purposes inside schools.

3

When Agendas Collide

The current environment in which education dollars are allocated to children in America's schools makes it nearly impossible to accomplish any single fiscal priority. In other words, just because a child living in poverty is sent extra funds from the federal government does not necessarily mean that the child receives a boost in education spending over a child from a more affluent family. Put very simply, as one hand giveth to the high-poverty child, the other hand taketh.

This process happens almost invisibly and incrementally, not because of a grand design but because of the fine print in state rules and labor contracts and idiosyncratic decisions by individuals who control resources. Small differences compound and accrue substantial dollar gains to some student types and losses to others.

In fact, the diffusion of education funding means no one governmental level takes full responsibility for funding any particular student type. Each level prioritizes different students and has different strategies for deploying resources. The result is a multilayered system in which the layers at times work at cross purposes.

Different players in the system have different agendas, which can influence how policies ultimately are implemented. Where funds originate at one governmental layer, the various influences in the fiscal system can and do work at cross purposes so the ultimate spending increments often bear no resemblance to what the policymakers intended.

When Federal and State Policies Are Distorted
by Local Implementation

This distortion is clear in the story of the Title I program. At its inception in 1965, policymakers were optimistic that infusing federal funds into poor schools would help break the cycle of poverty (see Jennings 2000).

Only four years into the implementation of the Elementary and Secondary Education Act, however, a report from the National Association for the Advancement of Colored People (NAACP) created a major controversy. It recounted scandalous misuse of Title I funds. After reviewing federal audits of states and school districts, the NAACP report charged that "Title I funds purchase services, equipment, and supplies that are made available to all schools in a district . . . even though many children reached are ineligible for assistance." In some cases, the report noted, "Title I funds are not going to eligible children at all" (McClure and Martin 1969, 5).

The report documented use of federal funds to purchase equipment and facilities for general use, acquisitions not contemplated in the statute. Even more troubling, Title I funds were occasionally used to buy band and sport uniforms or build swimming pools, sometimes in segregated schools that denied access to low-income minority children.

This report urged the federal government to enforce Title I's requirements for equalization of state and local resources between Title I and non–Title I schools and to "insure the proper use of Title I funds." The impact of these recommendations focused Title I legislation and regulations quite sharply. A key provision, "comparability," was added as the foundation of Title I funds allocation. To this day, this provision remains the basis of Title I funds distribution under No Child Left Behind.

The comparability requirement stipulates that school districts must equalize educational services purchased with state and local funds before Title I funds are brought into the mix. On its face, the comparability requirement is eminently sensible. Title I funds are to layer on top of an equitable distribution of services, so the federal dollars augment services for poor students, enabling them to overcome the disadvantages that result from poverty.

However, as figure 3.1 demonstrates, one cannot assume districts are following this requirement. In this district, schools with fewer poor students receive a larger base allocation ($3,005 per pupil) than schools with more poor students ($2,369 per pupil). Differences between lower- and

Figure 3.1. Targeted Federal Funding atop Uneven Base Allocations in One School District

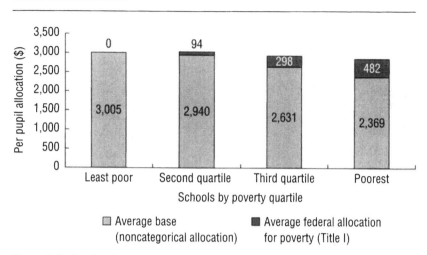

Source: Author's calculations based on analysis to Title I funding (Roza et al. 2005).

higher-poverty schools result from actual teacher salaries and the number of full-time-equivalent staff (FTEs) purchased; these contribute to inequities in the base allocation among schools within a district. Federal Title I dollars that disproportionately land on higher-needs students do not fully compensate for the inequities in the base allocation.

For the federal government, these patterns in base allocations directly counter its efforts to use funds to close the achievement gap. Where districts offset federal funds by disproportionately spending more discretionary funds on wealthier schools, the federally targeted dollars cannot possibly boost spending and student performance among the high-poverty schools. Put more simply, when the federal government invests funds to ensure that the highest-poverty schools have more resources, local governments counteract this investment by directing their resources disproportionately to lower-poverty schools.

In a different example, the federal government provides a fairly equitable sum for bilingual education. Yet, as can be seen in figure 3.2, districts augment federal dollars at different levels. Analysis of 2003 data reveals that students in Cleveland received additional local funds to the tune of $3,525 per student with limited English proficiency, whereas students in Solon received only $1,727 more than the federal allocation, and

Figure 3.2. Local Allocations Change the Effect of Federal Investments in Bilingual Education, Ohio

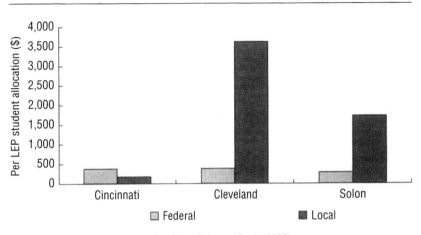

Source: Author's calculations based on Roza, Guin, and Davis (2008).

students in Cincinnati received only $177 (Roza, Guin, and Davis 2008). Again, different local policies dramatically altered the impact of the federal investment on different districts. If federal lawmakers intended that targeted bilingual education allocations level the playing field for these students, these findings beg the question, "Which students?"

The forces that reverse the effect of federal allocations work in the same way to distort state allocations (Roza, Guin, and Davis 2008). States also target funds to certain student programs (poverty, bilingual education, special education, gifted, and vocational education). Similar to the examples of local investments above, once state funds come into the district accounts, different priorities often emerge. These priorities create spending patterns across schools and districts that are not evident in state allocations.

Conflicting Agendas within a Single Level of Government

Conflicting agendas can emerge even within a single layer of government. Take for instance, Washington State's Learning Assistance Program (LAP). The program is a state allocation to districts with the intent of boosting spending on the state's poorest (and lowest-performing) students. The idea behind the allocation is to provide additional funds for poor students, *"particularly those living in concentrations of poverty."*

Yet, any time the legislature votes on new state allocations, a range of agendas ends up at the table. LAP was no exception. When interviewed about how the legislature decided on a formula for distributing the sizable allocation among districts, one legislative analyst reflected on what had happened:

> The committee was charged with devising a per pupil formula that would reflect poverty, concentrations of poverty, and student performance. We had what we thought was the perfect formula. We ran all the numbers showing how much each district would get. We had it all in a clean report with all the information on how and why we designed the formula. Problem was, when we brought that report back to the larger state legislature, each and every representative started out by thumbing through the report. They went right past the per pupil allocations. Then, they stopped when they got to the sums that their own district would get. That's when it all fell apart. It was so depressing. (Interview with CRPE staff, 2005)

The analyst went on to describe how a representative from a wealthy neighborhood argued that he could not accept a proposal that would bring his neighborhood's district such a small share of the funds. Others chimed in to request that each district (regardless of size, poverty level, and student performance) be guaranteed a fixed base amount. In the end, the legislature adopted an allocation formula that provided some minimum amount to each district, thereby ensuring that each representative could go back to his district and claim it as a win.

Figure 3.3 illustrates the effect of the revised allocation formula on the distribution across four of the state's larger districts. The district with the smallest share of poor kids received the largest per pupil LAP allotment. Bellevue School District received more than double the allocation per poor pupil than did the other three higher-poverty districts. The result is the opposite of the state's objective.

Local Implementation Completely Reversing Original Policy Intent

Figure 3.4 shows how federal, state, and local resources influenced spending for poor students across elementary schools in a large Texas district. Where federal dollars are concentrated primarily on schools

Figure 3.3. State-Allocated Poverty Funds per Poor Student, Washington

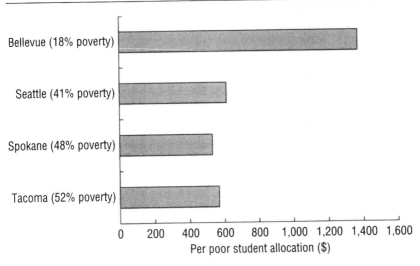

Source: Author's calculations based on Roza, Guin, and Davis (2008).

with higher proportions of students in poverty, state and local dollars are distributed in larger proportions to lower-poverty schools (often to ensure that all schools receive some benefit). Federally targeted funds, in this case, are not effective at providing the highest-poverty schools with a leg up. As was found in patterns on base allocations, when the federal government invests funds to ensure that the highest-poverty schools have more resources, local governments counteract this investment. In effect, local intentions work to ensure that all schools (regardless of poverty level) benefit in some way from all allocations.

Factoring in Labor Agreements

Nearly all education funding streams are ultimately converted into staffing costs, and teacher contracts play a big role in determining where and how the dollars are converted into staff administering student programs and services.

For instance, Delaware's Basic Education Formula allocates staff based on the number of qualifying students. The state reimburses the district for

Figure 3.4. Federal Funds Target High-Poverty Schools, While State and Local Funds Target Lower-Poverty Schools (by percent of poor students in each school)

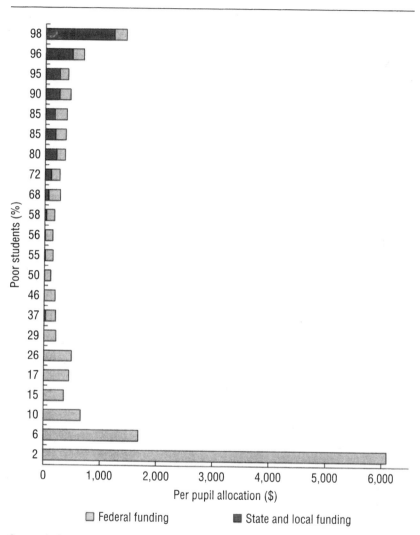

Source: Author's calculations based on Roza, Guin, and Davis (2008).

the actual costs of the staff hired using the labor contract's statewide salary scale. The amount of each district's allocation ultimately depends on the experience of the individuals hired, since that dictates where they land on the salary schedule. Districts with access to more experienced staff are awarded more money than those with access to less experienced staff—the opposite of what state lawmakers ostensibly intend. Here again, where state policy intends to fairly and equitably deploy funds for education, labor unions have a different agenda—namely, to represent the compensation preferences of their more influential and expensive members. Because the labor agreement dictates that funds convert into salaries as specified in the statewide schedule, the actual funds deployed favor schools able to hire more experienced teachers.

In another state, funds to boost achievement are used to reduce class size. The funds are used to hire and deploy new staff to lower class size evenly across the schools in the district. But when new staff are hired and compensated according to the negotiated salary schedule, fewer dollars are ultimately deployed to the children most in need of additional resources (figure 3.5).

While these examples demonstrate how labor contracts influence the flow of resources, additional research points out how labor agreements

Figure 3.5. Staff Salary Variations by School Assessment Ratings

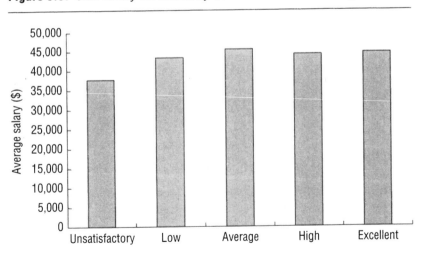

Source: Author's calculations based on 2005 data from a Colorado district.

prompt spending on items with little or no relationship to student learning. In other words, where increased student performance is the system's primary objective, labor agreements can produce spending that would suggest otherwise.

In an examination of eight common collective bargaining provisions with a weak or inconsistent relationship with student learning, CRPE finds that an average of 19 percent of every school district's budget is locked up by eight such provisions (Roza 2007b).[1] That translates to roughly $77 billion in annual public school spending nationally. Table 3.1 shows what the different contract provisions cost as a percentage of the average district operating budget. For instance, where labor agreements dictate teacher compensation systems where salary raises are largely based on longevity, the relevant research suggests very little if any relationship between longevity and student performance. Yet, as is indicated in the table, districts spend some 10 percent of their operating budgets on the incremental costs of these kinds of raises.

As stated in the *Frozen Assets* report (Roza 2007b), these funds clearly cannot be withdrawn from the public education system without affecting student learning. Rather, if student learning is the primary objective, the money might be spent differently and with greater effect. For instance, amid calls for incorporating merit-pay incentives into teacher compensation plans, a district might restructure its compensation system to

Table 3.1. The Total Cost of Common Teacher Contract Provisions

	Cost as a percent of school budgets
Teacher salary increases based on years of experience	10.01
Teacher salary increases based on education credentials and experiences	2.10
School days set aside for paid professional development	1.02
Above-average paid sick and personal days	0.52
Class size limitations	2.26
Mandatory use of teacher's aides	0.89
Above-average health and insurance benefits	1.28
Above-average retirement benefits	0.87
Total	18.95

Source: Roza (2007b).

direct some portion of the 10 percent spent on longevity to raises based on merit. One plan that would provide an additional $25,000 in compensation to 25 percent of all teachers and an additional $10,000 to another 25 percent of all teachers would increase that average school budget by $601 per pupil, or 7.25 percent.[2]

Or, the funds could be used to raise teachers' base salaries as a way to attract more and better teachers into the profession. A proposal by the National Education Association, for example, has called for a $40,000 minimum salary for all teachers (Winans 2005). Such a proposal would cost approximately $680 per pupil nationwide, or 8.2 percent of current school budgets. This is less than half of the resources currently tied up in common teacher contract provisions.

Teacher unions, like other forces mentioned in this chapter, are not solely responsible for the contradictory spending patterns described here. In fact, labor agreements require two signatures, one from labor and one from management, a fact often lost in debates about the impact of unions on public schools.[3] Similarly, as the next sections will show, school district officials, parents, principals, and other forces within the system play the roles they are given. Changing their roles means changing the system from top to bottom.

The Role of District Policies and Employees

Below the level of a district's central administrators, other decision-makers and special interests exert influence on allocations to various schools, some of which was explained in chapter 2. Often, individuals' roles in deploying resources or implementing programs create misalignment between the resource and the district's strategy. To illustrate how this works, consider a district that believes that one way to close the achievement gap is to provide more social services to disadvantaged students.

In one scenario (scenario 1), district leaders might choose to place a half-time social worker in every school to address this need. However, if the district's most disadvantaged populations are concentrated in a few of the district's larger schools, this allocation does not focus resources on high-needs students; it has the opposite effect. It creates a *smaller per pupil* investment in social workers in the larger, more disadvantaged schools where the resource is divided among a greater number of students.

Suppose instead that district leaders choose a second scenario (scenario 2) that creates a central pool of social workers, and principals are told to call on them when they see a need. In this case, the use of this resource depends entirely on how different principals use the service and in the way the social workers respond to the ebb and flow of demand. One principal with minor needs may monopolize social workers. A new principal might not be aware of her role in bringing in social services and may not call for these services all year. The distribution of social workers' time is ultimately driven by the actions of different players at the school level. In this case, it is difficult to predict whether the social workers' pool will actually benefit disadvantaged students.

In a third scenario (scenario 3), the district deploys social service "hours" to schools as a function of the number of disadvantaged students. Schools with higher numbers of disadvantaged students receive more total hours from social workers than schools with fewer disadvantaged students. This method concentrates the resources on the high-needs students.

These three scenarios are summarized in figure 3.6.

An analysis in one district (which provided the basis for this example) found that the district was relying on scenario 1. This district's vision statement purported that its paramount goal was to provide additional supports for low-performing students in order to close the achievement gap. In fact, this district relied heavily on per school allocations for many of its supports, not just social workers; 21 percent of all its allocations were driven out in per school allocations. Yet, allocation formulas driven *by schools* deliver equal increments for each school and thus effectively create higher per pupil allocations in smaller schools. Because this district's smaller schools had a smaller portion of high-needs students, the district ended up targeting more resources to less needy students—the opposite of the its stated strategy.

Analysis of districts regularly reveals inconsistencies between spending patterns and districts' stated strategies, many of which are the result of district staff choices about how to deploy resources to schools. In another example, a decentralized district with a commitment to equity deployed a large portion of funds based on staff discretion or demand from within the system. Yet when central staff decide how to deploy resources, schools *do not*. When schools do not make those decisions, the system is not decentralized, regardless of what the district strategy states.

Figure 3.6. How Some Resource Allocations Can Lead to Misalignment between Resources and Goals

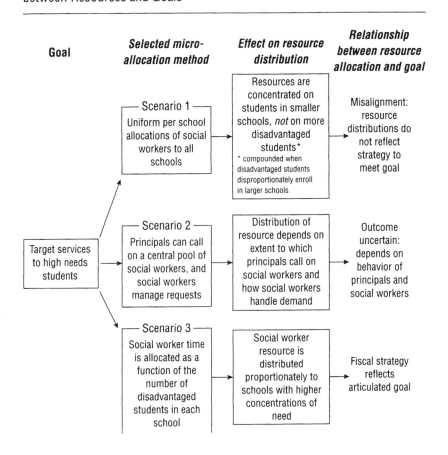

Conclusion

Allocation is a multistep process. And, as the numerous examples in this chapter demonstrate, leaks, diversions, and mixing occur at each step along the way. As a result, what trickles out on the other end often does not resemble what went in.

This chapter's findings point to major problems in the current manner of allocating funds to support stated improvement strategies. The exact nature of the problems differs somewhat from locale to locale, but what seems persistent is the notion that differences in agendas, formula details, local political forces, and other factors work at cross purposes. As a result, channeling dollars down to schools and students is anything but rational, coherent, or aligned.

Clearly, policymakers have not yet sorted out how to channel funds from one governmental level to the next so they ultimately reach the intended students. While the federal government may earmark funds for specific student types in order to boost spending at schools with high concentrations of those students, after these funds filter through state and local allocation streams, the end result may not be as intended. And as demonstrated here, those same forces work at odds with the intentions of allocations deployed from the state and even district headquarters.

Intentional, efficient, and coherent resource allocation policies have real consequences for schools. Chapter 4 details some ways in which these incoherent allocations are realized from the school vantage point.

4

Driving Blind

I t is an annual ritual in many urban school districts these days: figuring out where to nip and tuck the budget and how to spread the pain. While total enrollment in public elementary and secondary schools is expected to increase in 40 states through 2016, many urban districts and even entire states are struggling with how to "rightsize" their operations in the face of declining enrollments. Boston, New York, Philadelphia, D.C., Detroit, Cleveland, Cincinnati, Chicago, Minneapolis, St. Louis, Seattle, Portland, San Francisco, Oakland, and San Diego are among those districts grappling with menacing deficits arising from an imbalance between their revenues (which are linked to enrollment) and expenses.

What is worse, however, is that most district school boards and superintendents lack the financial tools necessary to pull together the data that would inform their cost-cutting strategies, especially at the school level. Despite extensive financial reporting requirements, most districts cannot answer basic questions that the public might have during these budget discussions: How much do remedial reading programs cost compared with tutoring? How much does the district spend on professional development, and how much would it cost if restructured? How much does the district spend on sports and electives? How much does Johnson Elementary receive relative to Lincoln Elementary? Of course, the sacred cows will have their constituencies to defend them, but the byzantine ways in which most districts track their spending defeat even the possibility of an honest evaluation of such questions and related opportunity costs. So the most obvious cuts are made—laying off staff, selling property, and cutting back on expensive services—simply based on the dollars and cents they appear to save.

The most damaging result of operating without reliable spending data across schools is that it undermines the goal of accountability under the No Child Left Behind Act. The federal law requires every school to be measured by student performance and imposes increasingly harsh sanctions for failing to meet performance benchmarks. But this focus on student performance by school and accountability is not aligned with resource allocation when some schools are given vastly more dollar amounts than others (none of which is reported in district reports).

District decisionmakers can use early efforts to develop an accurate, meaningful dashboard of indicators to inform their resource allocation and academic achievement goals. The challenges are many, but until district leaders recognize that their financial accounting systems are inadequate at the school level, they will continue to be "driving blind" and heading toward financial instability, even disaster.

Following the Dollars to Schools and Students

In truth, existing school district financial systems make it extremely difficult to trace most dollars appropriated to different students, schools, or strategies, fueling mistrust and thwarting reformers from building the case for necessary improvements. Most district financial practices intend to account for federal and state grants targeted at specific student types, such as low-income pupils. Budget officials assign expenditures that qualify for those restricted funds and, where needed, cover the additional costs of the services provided to these students out of the unrestricted operating fund. But, which schools the money goes to and to what end is hard to know. The answer to the seemingly simple question of "How much is allocated for bilingual education students at Eastside Elementary?" may require hours of analysis. If you ask this of district leaders, they will likely show you a thick board-approved budget that details spending by objects (e.g., teacher FTEs) and by programs or departments (e.g., elementary education, operations).

Researchers have sounded the call for improved financial tools to inform school district allocation in the past (Cooper 1993; Guthrie 1996).

Some have sought fiscal data disaggregated by schools for equity analysis (Fowler 2001; Goertz and Stiefel 1998). Others interested in the relationship between inputs and student outcomes have raised the need for entirely new accounting systems that track how resources are used in different school sites (Chambers 1999; Monk, Roellke, and Brent 1996; Odden et al. 2003). In response, several new accounting models have been created that specify how districts can code their expenditures to augment the quality of the fiscal data collected, including a "downward accounting extension" model (Fowler 2001), an accounting system to "reflect educational strategies" (Odden et al. 2003), a "resource cost model" (Chambers 1999), a "cost allocation model" (Miller, Roza, and Swartz 2005), and a "four-dimensional" financial model (Coopers & Lybrand, LLP 1994). Each accounting model is driven by different goals for research, analysis, accountability, or decisionmaking.

Where districts have adopted these new accounting models, the models yield more detailed school-level financial data, much of which is accessible via the web for entire districts and, in some cases, states (Texas and Minnesota, among others, report expenditure data by school on statewide reporting systems). Rather, the difficulty for interested district leaders is in how to *report* and *use* the school-based financial data for district leadership (Celio and Harvey 2005; Marzano 2000). With enrollments, programs, purchased resources, funding sources, and student needs varying across schools, district expenditure reports simply do not produce usable apples-to-apples spending comparisons across schools. Given the sheer volume of fiscal data that now exists, indicators are needed to inform leaders specifically about how investments vary across schools, types of schools, and types of students (Celio and Harvey 2005; Petrides and Nodine 2005).

Without function, there is no way to justify costs, understand them, or even respond sensibly to the fiscal chaos that shrinking enrollments cause for district budgets. District leaders typically react to the shrinking of available revenue by cutting programs, depleting reserves, imposing hiring freezes, and closing schools in order to reconcile the budget. For budget administrators, each program looks and feels like a fixed cost. Yet this is a mirage created by the very accounting systems upon which administrators rely.

Political lobbying fills the void of information: In one district, when budget cuts threatened to eliminate a nonformulaic music teacher, students playing instruments turned out en masse to school board meetings until the idea was abandoned. Staff positions, whether justified or not, become sacred and untouchable. Those principals who know how to work the system can often rake in the lion's share of these nonformulaic allocations. In one large district, without exception, the newest schools with no history working the system receive less per pupil than the rest of the district's schools.[1] In another analysis, while almost three-quarters of a district's revenues were tied to pupil counts, less than half of allocations were structured directly as a function of enrollment (figure 4.1). For district leaders trying to better manage their funds during enrollment shifts, managing their allocations in per pupil terms seems like a necessary requirement.

Many districts have started publishing school budgets tied to pupil counts, but most of these budgets offer only a partial and blurry view of school spending differences and may give the school's budget process a false impression of autonomy. Unlike charter, private, and parochial schools, which develop and manage their own budgets, individual public schools do not handle much money. Schools generally do not control any fiscal accounts, nor does the district set aside any real dollar figure for each school. Rather, as described earlier, district central offices hire staff and buy goods and services, which they then allocate to schools.

Figure 4.1. School District Revenues and Allocations by Funding Mechanism

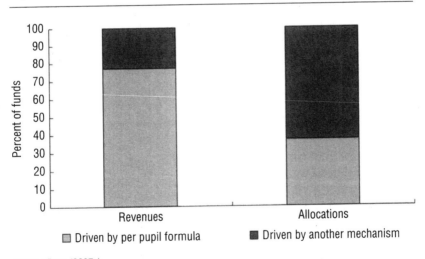

Source: Roza (2007c).

In one district studied for this book, the school board was determined to increase funding for middle schools, which it thought received less money than other schools. As CRPE researchers discovered, middle schools were already receiving more money per pupil than elementary and high schools, but the district did not know it. Another district proposed closing its small schools thinking they were more expensive, when in fact some were not.

Districts that do create individual school budgets are taking steps toward tracking a portion of their spending by school. In these places, the district then totals up the number of full-time-equivalent staff positions and converts them into dollars using districtwide average salaries for each type of staff. This approach has three major problems: the budgets fail to include the impact of central budget spending, they rely on average costs rather than actual costs, and they aren't stated in terms that are meaningful relative to a school's student population.

The first glaring problem is that where districts are computing school-based spending, these figures do not provide a complete picture of what is spent on each school. On average, school budget reports make up only 45 to 62 percent of a district's operating budget (Chambers 1999; Krop, Carroll, and Ross 1995). The remaining funds are in central budgets, most of which are reported and managed centrally and include, for example, programs for gifted students, teacher professional development, specialists, and the like. While some of this spending does not directly affect students (e.g., debt financing, Office of the General Counsel, and human resources), other spending represents supplemental funds or services that schools receive above and beyond those reported in the school budgets. In many cases, central spending ends up benefiting select schools more than others (e.g., special program staff, focused professional development, roaming specialists, truancy programs).

Central spending drives significant variation in school-level resources, yet districts have few ways to assess (or even coordinate) the distribution of these resources. Much of central spending is carved up and overseen by numerous departmental staff who create their own rules for distribution of their resources. For example, central budgets might fund a special art appreciation program in three schools, planetarium field trips for two schools, specialists instructed to respond to school requests, roaming therapists who can choose where to spend their day, and matching funds for elective teacher education costs.

Some analysts have tried to incorporate central spending into overall school spending figures by estimating average per pupil expenditures driven by central budgets (Chambers 1999). Unfortunately, this method does not capture school-to-school spending variability. Some districts have adopted new accounting frameworks that include school codes for various central expenditures, and others can trace staff assignments to specific schools and use these data to calculate, rather than estimate, how central budgets contribute to the relevant educational resources deployed to schools (Coopers & Lybrand, LLP 1994). Using one such framework, Miller and colleagues find that central budgets increase school spending by more than $2,601 per pupil, totaling a third of all resources received by the school (Miller et al. 2005). Of greater concern, though, is how different schools can benefit from these centrally administered resources. In a 2003 analysis of Denver public schools, some schools gained more than $4,000 when centrally administered resources were included, while another school in the same district benefited by less than $400.[2]

The second major issue with simply taking the gross number of school positions and calculating their cost using the districtwide average is that it conceals the true variance in spending between schools. As described earlier, the common practice of salary averaging—accounting for labor costs by using the average district salary for each school position rather than the real salary paid to individual employees—can greatly inflate, or deflate, the actual expenditures at any given school. As a result, two schools may appear to have the same per pupil budgets while, in reality, the district spends significantly more at the school with more experienced (and higher-paid) teachers. Take for example the two schools portrayed in figure 4.2. In 2003, Seattle's MLK Elementary was a high-needs school serving predominantly poor and non-English-speaking students. Seattle's Wedgwood Elementary was in a pricier neighborhood overlooking Lake Washington. In the bars on the left, which uses district-reported figures for total spending at the two schools, it appears that MLK received more funds. But when the district's average salary figure is replaced with the real salaries earned by the teachers at each school, the totals change to those on the right. In truth, the district spends less on MLK than on Wedgwood, despite district reports that portray the opposite.

As a 2002 analysis of Baltimore City showed, teachers at one high-poverty school were paid an average of $37,618, compared with over $57,000 at another school in the same district (Roza and Hill 2004). In the past five years, analysis from district after district has revealed the same

Figure 4.2. How Salary Averaging Obscures Funding Differences between Low-Poverty and High-Poverty Schools, Seattle

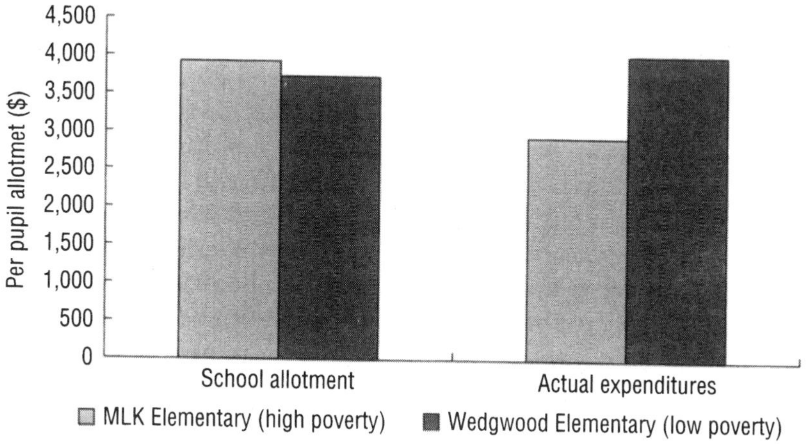

Source: Roza and Hill (2004).

patterns. Factoring out the value of real salary differences among schools in urban districts shifts school budget spending by up to 30 percent (Roza and Hill 2004).

Spending differences from school to school, after adjusting for salary averaging, are not random. As has been widely documented, teacher preferences dictate assignment in ways such that the greenest teachers generally serve in the most struggling schools (Education Trust–West 2005; Rose, Sonstelie, and Reinhard 2006). Thus, the real spending on a teacher in a high-poverty school is less than on the district's average teacher.

Confronted with this point, it is logical to ask why people care about salary differences when salary is so poorly connected with teacher effectiveness anyway. While it is true that longevity does not equate well with teaching effectiveness, the differences in average teacher salaries across schools indicate other problems inherent in the distribution of teachers. Schools with perpetually lower teacher salaries have high turnover among teachers. And turnover is related to school effectiveness. Further, schools with more senior teachers also enjoy large applicant pools for each teacher vacancy. Schools with very junior teaching staffs typically have only a handful of applicants for new teaching jobs, suggesting that they may not have access to the same quality of teachers as do the higher-spending schools.

By choosing to use only average salaries in district budgeting practices, these spending differences that shortchange high-poverty schools fly well below the radar.

Some researchers have accessed teacher and administrator salary data through district human resources and/or payroll departments and have incorporated these data within intradistrict analyses (Roza and Hill 2004; Stiefel, Rubenstein, and Berne 1998). Yet to date, most districts do not incorporate real salary costs into the school budgeting process.[3] Explanations for this omission differ, with some arguing that real salaries are a poor indicator of teacher quality and others pointing to accounting challenges.[4] With mounting evidence that high-poverty, high-minority schools receive the least experienced, lowest-cost teachers (Education Trust–West 2005), district leaders should be aware of real salary differences if they exist and the role such differences play in school spending comparisons.

The third major problem with estimating school budgets simply by using district average costs for their staff positions is that the resulting figures do not allow for comparison across schools with different student needs. Some revenues are driven by specific student needs with requirements that these funds are used only to augment spending for the identified students; thus, it is critical to take into account student need in spending comparisons (Fowler 2001). For example, when one school shows a relatively high per pupil spending average, district leaders may be left wondering if it is high enough given the school's student needs, too high, or only high because of added staff affiliated with a magnet program.

Take, for instance, two schools portrayed in the left bars in figure 4.3. Considering only the total spending, the district does spend more on the high-needs school: $5,000 per pupil versus $4,900 per pupil at the low-needs school. But the totals alone cannot differentiate whether differences among schools result from additional spending for the school's higher student needs, or school size, or extra base funding. By breaking the spending down further, particularly by how the funds are earmarked by student need (as shown in the bars on the right), it becomes evident that while the high-needs school receives more funds earmarked to address its students' needs, these funds offset the way the district shortchanges the school in base funding. In effect, the higher spending in the high-needs school may not be enough given the school's mix of student needs.

Unfortunately, most districts do not break out their school allocations to this level. To compare school spending usefully, districts need to account separately for allocations driven by student need.

Figure 4.3. How Earmarked Funds Affect Spending Comparisons between Low-Needs and High-Needs Schools

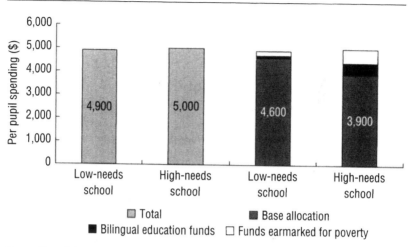

Source: Roza, Guin, and Davis (2008).

But with inadequate accounting mechanisms, producing these disaggregated fiscal data is no simple task. In 2005, reporters requested spending data from Chicago Public Schools for a story on how spending in predominantly African American schools compared to that in predominantly Hispanic schools. District leaders responded that such spending comparisons simply were not possible. The spending figures the district did provide combined costs for preschool, special education, and vocational education services, invalidating any spending comparisons across schools.

For the three reasons listed above, most districts operate without accurate or useful indicators of how spending compares across the schools within the district. The tragedy is numerous district decisions could (and probably should) be informed by school spending comparisons. For example, as districts experiment with new school designs (i.e., small schools, charter schools, virtual schools), spending snapshots are needed to signal whether such models are viable from a cost perspective. In one district studied, extra staff allocations for a Montessori focus in one school amounted to a 74 percent increase in spending over the district average.[5] Likewise, in another district, a recent decision to eliminate a

$300,000 program benefiting Latino students was made without recognition that the schools benefiting from the program were already shortchanged over $400,000 each year because of salary averaging (Roza 2005). These cost implications should inform district decisions about viable school designs and how to place resources across schools.

What Will It Cost to Bring High-Needs Students to Standard?

Educators and policymakers know that some students arrive at school without basic command of English, with disabilities, or from backgrounds of intense poverty, each of which poses unique challenges in helping those students meet performance standards. Educators and policymakers also know that these circumstances call for increased resources to enable all students to learn. Because of changing standards for what all kids should know and be able to do, many policymakers have become increasingly interested in the best approaches for structuring programs for students with identified needs. Logically, this step prompts questions about cost.

For example: how much will this new program for bilingual education students cost, and how does that compare with what the district is currently spending on these children?

Here again, policymakers at many levels operate in the dark with no reliable indicators of what districts are spending, how that compares to what is spent on high-needs students in other districts, or how much some proposed new program for these students will cost.

Some state policymakers have looked to revise fiscal policy to account for high-needs students in the funding formula. Specifically, they hope that the experts can tell them what to spend to ensure that a non-English-speaking student, a hearing impaired student, or a student with reading disabilities is able to reach the same level of proficiency as other children. And because performance goals are now a matter of law, it seems only reasonable that policymakers and researchers should know how much it costs to achieve them. The problem is, no one has a clue.

When policymakers and reporters ask researchers for such information, researchers find themselves repeatedly explaining that there is no industry standard for allocating a particular level of funding per pupil and that existing research on this question has yielded dramatically different figures for "what it would take" to enable different types of students to meet standards. They persist logically, hoping to at least learn from what other states or districts are doing. If there is no standard, they suggest, certainly there must be a list of what other localities are spending to educate students with identified needs.

The problem starts back at the individual district, which, again, lacks solid indicators on what it is spending on each student type. To date, most districts operate without reliable financial indicators that can clearly answer the question of how much is spent on a bilingual education student, or a student with learning disabilities, or a student with some other identified needs. With some of the money placed directly in school budgets, and some allocated to central departments that provide services for these students, districts have a hard time pulling together the right numbers to answer this key question.

But the question is an important one, and it matters at multiple levels of education strategy. At the district level, where leaders struggle with the right approach to serving students with different needs, comparisons of program cost must be taken in the context of how much is spent on existing programs. One district did not know it had cost issues until an outside analyst pointed out that the district was paying more than triple what was typical for treatment of a specific disability. In another urban district, district leaders negotiated class size limits for students with certain disabilities with its labor union, only to realize later that these class-size limits drove up costs well beyond what was typical elsewhere in the state for serving these students.

What Are the Trade-Offs?

Most of us are familiar with the concept of trade-offs in decisionmaking from personal financial choices. For instance, eating out several times a week can exceed the family budget. Yet, for districts, the budgets are so large that managing the hundreds or thousands of parts cannot be done intuitively. What is needed instead are solid, reliable accounting systems that inform resource allocation decisions.

Without the benefit of robust accounting systems that can offer accurate and meaningful fiscal data, education leaders frequently decide resources without understanding trade-offs. Acting without considering trade-offs invites everyone to lobby for their favorite thing with no discussion of the opportunity costs.

Take, for example, the ongoing debate about how best to stem the constant turnover of new teachers in some schools. To tackle the problem, some surveys have asked teachers what inducements would keep them in their roles. Interestingly, most such surveys report that reducing class size and improving working conditions were important, implying that salary may not be the most important ingredient. Yet, these surveys (and their resulting debates) took place in the absence of any real costs. Finally, in 2007, one research study computed a list of the cost-equivalent reforms below and surveyed teachers as to which they would prefer (Goldhaber, DeArmond, and DeBurgomaster 2007). It turns out that the vast majority of teachers prefers salary increases over many other reforms often proposed as a way to keep teachers, *once all reforms are put into cost-equivalent trade-offs.*

Table 4.1 displays the results. Teachers in Washington State were asked three questions. For each question, they were asked whether they would prefer a $5,000 raise over an alternative also priced at $5,000 for the district. So in the first question, teachers exhibited a preference for either a $5,000 raise or two fewer students in all the classes they taught. In each case, most teachers preferred the raise. Eighty-three percent preferred the raise to the equivalent spending on class size reduction, 88 percent preferred a raise over access to a teacher's aide, and 69 percent preferred a raise to more preparation time.

This study illustrates so nicely how decisions about how to use resources depend on understanding the cost-equivalent trade-offs. And yet, that is exactly what is missing in so much of school district financial decision-making.

Table 4.1. Teachers' Preferences for Annual Pay Increases versus Workplace Change among Cost-Equivalent Reforms

	Prefer a $5,000 increase (%)	N
Two fewer students in all the classes you teach	82.70	3,066
A new full-time teacher's aide who splits time between your class and four other teachers at your school	88.04	3,057
3.5 more hours of preparation time each week	69.34	3,056

Source: Goldhaber et al. (2007).

Take, for instance, the proposal by one education writer that public education ought to be spending triple what it currently spends for high-poverty students to close the achievement gap (Rothstein 2004). In real dollars, for a district that currently spends an average of $10,000 per pupil (which is fairly close to the current national average), triple that would be $30,000 per poverty pupil (or an increment of $20,000 extra for being poor). Now picture a family with three kids, and that increment effectively becomes $60,000 extra *per year* for being poor. Here is where a cost trade-off becomes relevant. Decisionmakers can imagine a scenario where the school system spends this extra $60,000 for additional services for these three students or simply gives that $60,000 to the poor family, immediately lifting it well out of poverty.

In another example, teacher salary increments for experience account for just over 10 percent of a given district's operating budget (Roza 2007b). This is a hefty price tag on an item with very little measurable link to student performance. In other words, while teacher salaries steadily increase during their careers, their effectiveness with students does not increase on a similar trajectory.[6]

School districts could, however, spend their dollars differently, perhaps reshaping compensation either to raise salaries for all teachers or to provide salary increments based on teaching effectiveness. Here again, examining the cost-equivalent trade-offs is important to see what is at stake. The dollars currently spent on automatic wage increases for longevity amount to 54 percent of all salary dollars, which, if so structured, could bring sizable wage increases to highly effective newer teachers who would otherwise need to wait decades for such rewards.

In another such example from the same study (Roza 2007b), the costs are computed for the unusually generous health benefits typically awarded to teachers. If teachers instead received health benefits comparable to professionals in other fields, the savings would amount to $1,900 per teacher. While some teachers might still prefer the health benefits over the extra dollars in salary or some other form, other teachers might opt for an equivalent salary increase. Here again, without considering the trade-offs, districts cannot even begin to make strategic decisions about how best to use money. But these kinds of trade-offs are rarely discussed, let alone priced out rigorously to encourage their consideration.

In one analysis of comparable districts in a region, the costs of providing building security varied from $9 per pupil in one district to $63 per pupil in a similar district. Had the second district reduced its costs to make them comparable on a per student basis, it would save over $3 million. In fact, when faced with these data, the second district cut its security budget dramatically.[7]

Conclusion

How can local leaders, and even constituents, operate without recognizing the implications of their spending patterns across schools and of other trade-offs? The most important answer is that *they don't know* about real spending patterns and, in many cases, are wrong about what schools are getting the most money. Bad information leads to mistaken assumptions and ultimately misguided strategic resource decisions.

5

What Does It All Mean for Schools?

Education finance headlines almost never include schools. Rather, Americans are much more likely to read about district, state, and federal financial swings. We hear about districts in financial turmoil, or state education budget increases, or approved federal budgets for education. But the public almost never thinks about education finance at the level of the school (unless to report a school closure). And yet, these other organizational levels exist only to support schools. Schools are where the learning occurs, not at the district headquarters, at the state capitol, or in federal agencies. So it makes sense to think about the effect of America's education finance system on *schools*.

From the school perspective, the questions go much deeper than "How much are we spending?" Rather, what seems more relevant is "Why do we spend our money this way? Who made these decisions? What is the strategy at hand? And how do fiscal decisions support our priorities?" This chapter takes stock of the kinds of answers that emerge when schools pose these questions.

Schools Make Very Few Decisions about Resource Use

In the 1980s, a popular reform idea enhanced the school-level dialogue on education finance. The reform was decentralization, and it empowered individuals and groups at the building level to play a more active role in education decisions. What it did not do, however, was hand over any real resource decisions to schools (Hansen and Roza 2005). Most would consider the reform ineffective in leveraging any meaningful change (Bimber 1994), but the conversations that took place at schools about resources have lasted.

Principals and school site councils still meet to talk about what is going on at the schools. In many of these conversations, attendees talk about what can and cannot be done at the school level, and what schools might or might not expect from district headquarters next year. In one school's parent club meeting the author of this book attended last year, the principal pointed out, much to the disappointment of many parents in the room, that the school would not know for a while whether it would be keeping its school counselor position. But, this school was eligible for class size reduction and might also receive more teacher release time. Parents voiced their preference for the counselor over the other reforms. The principal openly agreed but said it was out of her hands, as these were things being decided "downtown."

In truth, the push for more release time was coming from the district's professional development office to support a districtwide initiative, and the class size reduction funds were coming from a state legislature decision. But, more important, what the conversation illustrates is exactly where decisions about resources *are not* being made: at the schools.

Rather, as the previous chapters demonstrate, decisions about resource use are made by many actors and at many different levels of the system, so very few, if any, resource decisions are controlled at the school site. This reality generated confusion in a CRPE interview with one principal in a larger district. The researchers' broad task was to determine how well resources were aligned with academic priorities; as such, they incorporated that question into interviews conducted with school principals. When asked how resources at her school were aligned with academic priorities, the principal responded:

> Well, I try to encourage the teachers to use our money for field trips or supplies that the teachers believe will help support their work. And, you know, when I get

a request for something and it sounds fishy, I'll come back to the teacher with some questions about what it's for.

The CRPE researchers followed up by asking specifically about how resources in the form of staff allocations reflected academic priorities, at which point she said:

> Oh! I thought you meant our school budget. We get $4,000 from the district for our school-based budget and that's what I use for field trips and supplies. Now on staff positions, we don't have any input in what the district does with our staffing. We get what we get in terms of teachers and other positions.

For this school, the $4,000 in discretionary funds represented less than one-half of 1 percent of what was actually spent on site in teacher salaries and other direct costs for the school. The reality for most schools is that they have little, if any, input into how resources are used in their schools.

More recently, a handful of districts, including those in Houston, Oakland, New York City, Chicago, and Boston, have implemented various decentralization efforts that come with some school-based autonomy over resource decisions. These new arrangements on behalf of the districts allow some or all schools in the district to participate more actively in real spending decisions. Yet even when the district supports school-based resource decisions, schools still have to abide by state prescriptions, federal rules for federal grants, local levy promises, and labor contracts. So while some schools might be able to trade a counselor for an art teacher, many trade-offs cannot be considered for fear of bumping up against the rest of the system. In Delaware, one analysis estimates that 83 percent of each district's budget is inflexible at even the district level (Boston Consulting Group 2007). In other words, even if the district passed on all its flexibility to schools, Delaware schools would only be able to control some 17 percent of the funds awarded to them.

So from the school level, when people ask who makes resource decisions, it becomes clear that individuals, leaders, groups, and forces outside the school building are largely responsible. With so many cooks, it is no wonder that the pot is so unsavory. In effect, the education finance system operates without any locus of control.

And that poses a contradiction for one of the cornerstones in state and federal education reform: namely, that of school-based accountability. Simply put, federal and state policies are designed to hold schools accountable for student performance, yet decisions about resource use are mostly made anywhere but at the school. Instead, resource decisions are determined by federal, state, and district officials, with influence brought to bear by powerful labor unions, voter groups, and other special interests.

Schools Are on Anything but a Level Playing Field

The education finance system not only ensures that few, if any, decisions about resources are made at the school level, but it also enables a system that provides wildly different dollar allocations to different schools in the same district.

Together, the budgeting practices described in earlier chapters can lead to significant differences in spending from one school to the next. In a 2003 analysis of spending patterns in Denver, the district spent over $14,000 more per pupil in one school than in another.[1] A 2004 analysis uncovered a high school in Chicago in which the district spent over five times as much per pupil as it does for another. While these examples are particularly extreme, over the years, CRPE researchers have uncovered spending disparities of more than $5,000 per pupil among selected schools within Austin, Seattle, Baltimore, Fort Worth, and other urban districts, generating over hundreds of thousands (and at times, millions) of dollar differences in total spending at the school level (Roza 2003; Roza, Guin, et al. 2007).

One thing is clear: The amount spent on any one type of child—say a non-English-speaking student—varies tremendously within a district depending on what *school* the child attends. Unlike spending variations across districts, variations within districts have nothing to do with access to resources. They have to do with staffing patterns, choices about where particular programs are placed, special staff assignments, and other oddities of allocation practices.

While many of these disparities are not easily apparent, the flip side is that schools cannot clearly see what level of resources they are receiving relative to other schools. The opaque spending policies fuel not only inequity, but also mistrust. What is more, they invite influence. More savvy school leaders know how to work the district system and can often leverage their influence to their benefit. Other schools see that the squeaky wheel gets the grease, and they try to squeak too.

Here again, local reality contradicts accountability reforms brought on by state and federal reforms. In the case of accountability legislation that holds schools accountable for student performance, success undoubtedly hinges upon equitable allocation of resources. Yet, district budgeting practices do little to ensure that schools have access to similar resource levels and mask the resources they actually receive. Current budgeting practices that yield erratic spending differences among schools certainly undermine efforts to hold all schools to the same standards.

The Finance System Works Against a Coherent and Efficient Strategy for Improvement

School leaders often voice good ideas about how to best serve their students in their unique context. More often than not, those ideas do not fit with the reform ideas of the numerous other players in the system deciding how resources are to be used.

Take, for instance, one of the many schools to receive funds from the Bill and Melinda Gates Foundation for its proposal to capitalize on the small high school concept. This Washington State school sought to provide more personalized learning experiences for all its students, largely through redefining the specialized roles of its staff into more generalized positions that could help students with all their needs. The school's principal said in an interview that district and state policies conflicted with the school reform model at every turn. Minimum staffing allocations for each school forced the hire of some specialists, while the model hinged on generalists. District teacher professional development trainings, designed for 50-minute periods, conflicted with the block scheduling the school had adopted. Even the district's grounds, maintenance, and custodial policies were at odds with the design, since the district-run department sent out different building maintenance staff each day instead of accommodating the school's plea for a single adult that could know the students by name.

Because the funds arrive to districts in so many different pots, each with its own restrictions on how funds can be used, the services brought to bear on schools are often fragmented, with multiple programs and services for each type of student. The fragmentation of funding restricts schools (and districts) from deciding how best to meet the needs of their students. In South Carolina, for example, funding for a new school design might draw on some of the state's 25 separate categorical allocations earmarked for alternative schools, junior scholars, youth in government, homework centers, and others that can be used as a way to fund the school. But some of these allocations are intended only for math and science schools, or schools for arts and humanities, or "lab schools," or SAT improvement. Some funds are earmarked for operating costs, while others can be applied only for personnel. Some are intended only for special services (like character education or alcohol abuse services). As a result of all these restrictions, creating a new innovative school means piecing funds together into a patchwork quilt that may or may not have any coherence (Hassel and Roza 2007).

At the school level, building leaders are quick to point out the contradictions under which they work. One principal explained that his state provides funding for summer school, but since many of his school's students are employed in the local resorts' tourism industry in the summer, most cannot take part. For this school, restricting funds for use on summer assistance makes little sense. The school would undoubtedly achieve better results with these students by using the funds for a Saturday program during the school year. But the funds are not transferable, and no provision is made for local context.

In another school, the district continues to provide bus transportation to all students to the school, despite the fact that more than half could safely walk. The principal wants to redirect the funds to other services but says the district cannot, since those funds are earmarked by the state for transportation only.

And so it goes. The view from the school shows just exactly how the finance system works to perpetuate fragmented services, incoherent strategies, and inefficient use of funds.

Money Is Not Where the Mouth Is

In the opening chapter of a textbook on public budgeting, the authors cite the importance in figuring out where the funds are going: "An organization's resource allocation system is a manifestation of the organization's strategies, whether those strategies are the result of thoughtful strategic planning process, of the inertia of long years of doing approximately the same thing, or of the competing political forces within the organization bargaining for shares of the resources" (Lee, Johnson, and Joyce 2004, 3). In other words, the allocation of funds reveals the system's implicit strategy, regardless of what official proclamations state about what is important, what the goals are, and so forth.

Nowhere is that contradiction more apparent than amid the resource allocation patterns the CRPE team has uncovered in schools. Consider the standard education policymaker mantra versus the reality evident in the distribution of dollars in schools. Box 5.1 lines up typical statements with a relevant spending reality for each. As the box indicates, the spending realities presented here directly contradict the stated priorities evident in everyday education leader statements. So where the public hears about efforts to close achievement gaps between minorities and white students or between higher-performing and lower-performing students, in truth different parts of the finance system are directly at odds with those stated objectives. Paying higher salaries for teachers in low-minority schools or spending more on honors classes would suggest just the opposite.

As the previous chapters indicate, the sources of the contradictory spending patterns are buried deep in different elements of the finance system, controlled by different parties with different agendas, and all intertwined in such a way that unraveling one piece is unlikely to alter the final result. Take, for instance, the fact that many high schools spend

---

Box 5.1. Stated Strategies Do Not Match Strategies Implicit in Spending

Standard education leader mantra:	*Reality evident in school spending:*
We are trying to close the achievement gap between whites and minorities.	On average, districts employ less expensive teachers to teach minority students than whites.
We are doing everything we can to help give poor students a leg up.	Districts spend a greater share of unrestricted district funds on nonpoor students than on poor students.
Our focus is on getting students up to speed in core subjects.	Schools spend more per pupil to offer courses in electives than courses in core subjects.
We are diverting more resources to help the lower performers.	Schools spend more per pupil for an honors or AP course than for regular or remedial courses.
We are trying to prepare our students for a role in our changing economy.	Schools spend more per pupil to participate in ceramics and basketball than in math or science.

more per pupil on a ceramics class than on a math class. The computation is a fairly simple calculation, dividing the teachers' salaries across their teaching responsibilities, and then dividing further by the course enrollment. So because math classes tend to be larger than elective classes and are more often taught by junior teachers—schools turn over more math teachers than those with other certifications, so salaries are perpetually lower—the per pupil costs for electives can be double or triple that for math classes.

However, it is not just class size and salary. High school schedules that divide the day evenly among all courses (with ceramics meeting for the same number of minutes as math) are also part of the problem.

Yet try to change any of these factors to alter the spending patterns, and the system constraints are immediately apparent. Teacher salaries are highly protected by powerful labor unions. When Washington State's governor Christine Gregoire tried to introduce a statewide bill to offer bonuses to math and science teachers as a way to recruit and retain more teachers with this expertise, the bill fell apart in the face of resistance by the Washington Education Association—the state affiliate of the National Education Association.

Changing school day schedules is not much easier. Cutting into ceramics to allow for more time in math can pose problems for students using the elective to earn credits toward graduation. And perhaps even more problematic, changing the schedule shrinks the workload for the ceramics teachers and increases it for the math teachers, creating the need to reshuffle the high school faculty when math teachers are already in short supply.

Instead, the system perpetuates, and the policies, practices, and habits that sustain the seemingly immovable inertia of the public education finance system continue virtually unchanged, regardless of the mantra.

So, taking the above quoted textbook statement at face value, that resource allocations are the implied strategy, one could argue that the implicit strategy inherent in spending realized at the school level is one where the system

- is trying to increase the gaps between minorities and whites;
- supports the notion that for students to be successful in life, they must master electives first and core subjects second;
- reinforces the benefits realized by wealthier students;
- is working to expand the achievement gap between high and low performers; and

- is betting that the key to employment in a changing economy stems from building skills in ceramics and other electives, not math and science.

These are the implicit priorities evident in the existing spending patterns at the school level.

Dollars, but No Sense

When making the case to a room full of education policymakers that the system is not spending our dollars in ways consistent with our stated mantra, the author of this book is now accustomed to the predictable response that nearly always comes next from at least one attentive listener. The problem with this argument, the listener says, is that the actual dollar expenditures are a poor indicator of what is actually delivered to each school.

And yes, that is true. In our current system, the dollar expenditure for any teacher, program, school, service, or other input does not reflect the inherent value of that input for students.

Take for example, the costs of a reading program implemented in two different schools. Depending on a host of implementation details, the characteristics of the adults involved, local capacity issues, and other dynamics inherent in the system, the program could add huge value in one school and very little value, *even if the dollar expenditure is the same,* in the other.

Or, consider the costs of a second grade teacher at two different schools. While one might be $40,000 and another might be $80,000, the price difference by itself does not indicate the relative value of each. This higher-salaried one might be more effective, or both might be equally effective, or the lower-salaried one could be much more effective than the other. There is absolutely no way to know based on the salary alone.

So how did the connection between dollars and the value of what is provided become severed? Here is how. Dollars are allocated from one governmental level to the next, each imposing prescriptions and regulations. Districts are then tasked with disseminating staff, services, and programs (not dollars) out to schools. Salary schedules, organizational habits, and longstanding commitments to system staff, community stakeholders, program officials, and service providers then work to convert the dollars into what is ultimately realized at the school level.

Because district leaders know that the dollars do not mean much, they do not use dollars as an important indicator in making strategic resource allocation decisions. Instead, districts allocate FTEs, programs, and services, often reporting costs with the average salaries and not the real ones. Ultimately, those doing the allocating are forced to focus more on meeting the requirements to staff schools and expending funds in ways consistent with all the rules and commitments made than on getting good value for the dollar.

So it is true that the dollars do not reflect the actual value of what is realized in the school. That is why district leaders don't put much stake in them. But if dollars cannot indicate the value of resources across schools, what can?

Some might suggest that staff FTEs are a better currency and that policymakers should work to ensure strategic and equitable allocation of FTEs, not dollars. But, as others inevitably point out, FTEs are not particularly reliable either. One school might be staffed with top-notch experienced and dedicated teachers that work well together to best meet the needs of their students. Meanwhile, another may have a revolving door of junior teachers under poor building leadership, no mentorship, and programs that are mismatched for its student population. Numbers of FTEs will not pick up on these real differences either.

What does matter? Here the research is clear. Numerous studies of effective and ineffective schools have nearly uncovered the nonmonetary factors that add value for schools. Typically, effective schools use data to inform practice, have good leadership, have more dedicated and committed teachers, provide extra help for struggling students, and set high goals. The problem is that none of these things is monetized in the education finance system.

One way to think about these other factors is to consider them a "resource" for schools. While clearly a nonfinancial resource in the current model, they represent important inputs that are brought to bear in the schooling process. The thing is, the system could monetize these inputs, but it does not. Education could pay more for higher teacher motivation, effective principal leadership, attention to data, and a coherent plan for improved achievement. These could be monetized inputs, and policymakers could restructure the purchasing system to capture them more deliberately.

Recognizing these factors as resources implies that the current purchasing model is not paying for what matters. The question should not be what is the best indicator of the real value of the resources, but rather how to better link the dollars and these valuable nonmonetary resources so they are strategically deployed across schools and systems.

Instead, districts operate with a poor sense of the inherent value of their resources, assuming (hoping) that the distribution makes sense, when in fact it does not even come close. It is an enormous flaw in the existing system that the dollars are poorly connected to the value of what is delivered to schools.

Conclusion

Once researchers are down deep in schools, it becomes clear that the finance system is performing poorly. School leaders are dealt a deck that makes it impossible for them to decide anything of relevance, and yet the accountability system aims to measure student progress school by school. Decisions about resource use, including staff assignments, programs, and service delivery models, are all imposed by forces outside the schoolhouse. What reaches the schools is inequitable, thus further rendering school-based accountability meaningless. The resources are provided in ways that prohibit a coherent, efficient strategy for improvement. And the end result is spending that directly conflicts with America's most basic objectives for education reform.

6

A Wicked Problem
Why Typically Proposed Overhauls of the Finance System Are Guaranteed to Fail

In response to the recognized problems with America's current system of education finance, policymakers have proposed and attempted several solutions, including making efforts toward "adequacy," modifying state and federal regulations and prescriptions, decentralizing decisions about resource use to schools, and imposing accountability for outcomes. Instead of solving the problems, these actions have pushed the system into even greater trouble. The critical flaw in each case is that while the proposed solution tinkers with some problematic element of the system, it leaves another problem intact. In the end, no one proposed solution will remedy the entire package of incoherent, inefficient, and inequitable spending. In some cases, the proposed solution actually aggravates some of these issues.

As this chapter demonstrates, single-dimension solutions implemented by one level in the system will not solve the complex problems brought on by the multilevel school finance system. Each proposed finance overhaul or remedy is flawed and incomplete, and each contributes to what is now becoming what German theorist Horst Rittel would call a "wicked problem."

The Wicked Problem

Horst Rittel was a professor of design and social planning at the University of California, Berkeley. He worried about ill-conceived design and planning efforts to solve messy and circular problems, which he tagged as "wicked," in contrast to the relatively straightforward problems in such subjects as mathematics and chess. Rather than having a clear-cut, correct answer, wicked problems are extremely complicated.

America's school finance system exhibits many characteristics of a wicked problem: it is a house of cards, and any effort to dismantle or overhaul one piece will always require a new prop.

Jeff Conklin, a computer scientist at the Microelectronics and Computing Consortium in Austin, Texas, wrote a book defining wicked problems and their characteristics in 2006. Conklin explains that with wicked problems, one cannot see the scope of the problem from any one vantage point. Indeed, there is often no definitive statement of "the problem." There are so many factors and conditions, all embedded in a dynamic context, that no two wicked problems are alike, and the solutions to them will always be custom designed.

Unlike the challenge of calculating return on investment or making sense of numbers on a spreadsheet, wicked problems have incomplete, contradictory, and changing requirements. They involve complex interdependencies. Solving one aspect of the problem reveals or creates other, sometimes even more complex, problems. One characteristic that defines a wicked problem is that solving it requires large numbers of people to change their attitudes and behaviors, such as in the case of environmental issues. With such a large-scale and widespread problem as the deterioration of the environment, it is necessary that large groups of people (i.e., citizens of a city, state, country, or even of the globe) be on board to attempt a comprehensive solution.

Another characteristic of wicked problems is that competing stakeholders have different views of what needs to be done. This characteristic comes to light most clearly in such areas as transportation. Many people have a stake in how transportation is developed and managed, and people have just as many different opinions on how transportation issues should be handled. Each person or group involved adds complexity that increases the wicked factor.

Most proposed solutions to a wicked problem provide a "one-shot operation," and each attempt has its consequences. The catch-22 is that one cannot learn about the problem without trying solutions, but every solution is expensive and has lasting, unintended consequences, which are likely to spawn new wicked problems.

The different layers of the school finance system provide some essential ingredients of a wicked problem. Because so many decisionmakers are involved in what ultimately are inefficient and inequitable allocations, the path to a solution is unclear. The "competing stakeholders" do not share the same view of a coherent finance system, and there is no easy way to break through the tangle of opinions and come up with a viable solution.

Because of the risky nature of wicked problems, reformers must be extremely cognizant of the limitations and dangers of proposed solutions. As this chapter explains, solutions that have already been proposed and implemented have added their own complications to the wicked problem of school finance.

Proposed Strategies for Education Finance Reform Offer Incomplete Solutions

Proposals for education finance reform have sprung up similarly in nearly every state. While some of these proposals may improve part of the system, none of the solutions they offer comprehensively fixes the wicked problems of school finance.

The Adequacy Proposal: Increase Spending

Over the past decade, nearly all states have considered increasing education revenues toward reaching some "adequate" spending level. The logic behind the movement is that with more funds, the education finance system can more effectively meet all the needs of students, and therefore state lawmakers should increase spending to some adequate level.

Adequacy lawsuits are often brought on behalf of the poor and disadvantaged students served by urban public school systems. Plaintiffs argue that disadvantaged students cost more to educate, and unless the districts that serve them receive extra money, education of the disadvantaged will be underfunded. These plaintiffs presume that school districts are able to use additional funds effectively and target them accordingly to high-needs students.

As has been detailed in earlier chapters, the truth is that urban school districts do not effectively target their existing funds to high-needs students and often fail to direct funds to what they have identified as high-priority functions. Researchers have seen how district policies direct a smaller share of unrestricted dollars for the education of disadvantaged students than for the education of others. They have seen how undocumented practices spend a great deal of money on some schools, while other schools in the same district are shortchanged. In reality, spending varies significantly from school to school within a district, driven not by policy or strategy but by budgeting practices that accommodate teacher preferences, political forces, and haphazard distribution of a multitude of uncoordinated programs and services.

Yet, as Americans are now finding, simply infusing more money into the system provides absolutely no guarantee that the new funds will land on those students that are currently shortchanged. In fact, given what researchers know about how district allocation practices work, they should assume that new funds will follow the same path as existing funds and therefore will not help address the many inequities and inefficiencies inherent in the finance system. A historical view of education spending suggests that the system is now spending its money in the same ways and on the same things as it always has, just in larger quantities and at much greater cost. Increasing the overall pie changes none of the dynamics in the system. Thus, this solution does not tackle many of the problems outlined in the last chapter.

Where districts do in fact have access to more money, there is little evidence to suggest that the funds are applied in ways that fundamentally address inequities. Rather, new funds are often directed to raise salaries, reduce class sizes, or increase electives (McNeil 2007; Roza and Hill 2006). The problem is that these investments in no way change the dynamics of the school finance system and are unlikely to counter the forces that work to the advantage of some students. Further, changes in salaries are across the board and do nothing to target resources to high-needs students. Consequently, they are unlikely to close the achievement gap in any way.

While each new investment sounds positive as a standalone, these state changes further restrict schools from making the decisions most appropriate for their students. While the flurry of activity provides some sense of solving education finance challenges, it does nothing to address the critical dimensions of the larger wicked problem.

Further, simply layering on new funds will likely reinforce the existing spending patterns among schools. A recent adequacy calculation from Illinois suggests that the state should be spending $2.2 billion more than it currently spends, amounting to just over a $1,000 increase in spending per pupil. Yet, in taking stock of inequities among Chicago schools, researchers found that the system already spends more than the new target amount on 67 of its schools (Roza and Hill 2006). New funds brought into the existing resource allocation system will undoubtedly result in even higher spending for these 67 schools, while others still will not receive enough funds to meet the target. Americans cannot assume that new funds will create comparable boosts in spending at all schools.

Because the adequacy movement has now been around for several years, some evidence of these disappointing predictions is starting to surface. In Arkansas, for example, lawmakers have increased school funding by $700 million since 2003. Although school finance consultant Larry O. Picus recommended using funds for instructional coaches, smaller class sizes, and tutors for students at risk of failing, legislators did not insist that expenditures match these recommendations (McNeil 2007). As a result, new expenditures in the Arkansas school system took the following form: increased teacher salaries, larger than recommended class sizes, new administrative hires, new electives, and less than adequate numbers of additional tutors. As was no real surprise, while student performance improved, it did not reach expectations. The problem, of course, is that adequacy reforms leave the districts' decisionmaking processes intact, making it likely that additional funds will follow the same patterns as current funds (Roza and Hill 2006).

Adequacy solutions also face a technical flaw. That is, the solution is premised on the notion that an "adequate" funding level can be determined with inputs based on the flawed finance system currently in place. Here is how it works: The dollar amount is to be computed based on one of a handful of approaches, all of which draw on current spending in some way as an input. In one method, experts determine a list of desired inputs and then "cost out" those inputs, using the system's costs to convert those desired inputs into a total dollar figure. In another method, statistical analysis is used to project spending needed to achieve desired outcomes based on the current relationship between spending and outcomes. Others use somewhat different strategies, but they all draw on some fiscal element of the existing system in their calculations. The problem? Any dollar figures drawn from the existing finance system are suspect.

One key failing in the current education finance system is in how the system converts dollars to resources. As described in the last chapter, the real dollar expenditure each school receives has very little bearing on the inherent value of what is delivered, and that means that dollar measurements extracted from the current system should not be used to craft solutions.

While adequacy calculations differ in their approach, their data, and ultimately their determinations, determining what amount of resources is adequate depends highly on how the resources will be used. There is no way for policymakers to assess the cost effectiveness of new schooling models without accurate cost estimates.

Centralize Spending Decisions: Proposals for Greater State Prescriptions on Spending

Some state legislators are pursuing the idea of increasing state prescriptions on resource use, while at the same time, others are considering the exact opposite: lifting constraints on state funds. Both proposals are pitched as ways to address criticisms of multilevel decisionmaking, but they essentially opt for different levels in the system to take control.

Proposals to centralize more spending decisions to the state level take different forms. Some suggest providing funds to districts with the stipulation that the funds be used to adopt promising programs. Others try to standardize key spending decisions by establishing minimum class sizes. Some states have fielded proposals to prescribe a "65 percent solution," where districts must use 65 percent of their resources on the classroom, and policies where the state dictates some portion of state funds (defining class size, school staffing patterns, program and services, and so on). More recently, states have proposed imposing a school staffing model derived from best practice research on effective schools.

The logic behind such proposals is twofold. First, districts cannot be trusted to distribute funds equitably and fairly across schools. So it follows that taking charge of resource allocation decisions at the state level would counter local forces that work to shortchange needier students. Indeed, state lawmakers are increasingly faced with evidence of district spending practices that favor wealthier students over high-needs students. Take, for example, a study by the Public Policy Institute of California that shows how high-poverty elementary schools in California receive a smaller share of unrestricted funds, some of which was made up for with state and federal targeted dollars (Rose et al. 2006). Table 6.1 summarizes the data from the report.

Findings such as these prompt state lawmakers to consider proposals to earmark a greater share of funds to force districts to spend those funds in certain ways on high-needs students.

The second part of the logic behind increased state prescriptions stems from evidence that district-level problems are not only with how funds are distributed, but also with what is purchased. Compilations of research on the relationship between inputs and outcomes provide new insights on what investments are more likely to yield positive outcomes for students (Odden 2007). Yet policymakers see that districts do not necessarily apply their resources in the ways this research implies. Take, for instance, Arkansas, where evidence showed that when new funds were applied, districts did not spend those funds on promising items but rather put the funds to such items as increased elective offerings. As the reasoning goes, state policymakers are better consumers of education research and are thus better able to turn that evidence into policy prescriptions that, while not a perfect fit in all cases, can improve overall effectiveness and efficiency.

That said, centralizing spending decisions to the state creates several problems. First, states have not necessarily fared better than districts in creating defensible resource allocation patterns. As data in chapter 2 showed, politics playing out in one state legislature directed a larger proportion of funding for disadvantaged students to wealthier districts.

Second, moving more decisions about resource use to the state can create inefficiencies and stifle innovation. Take, for example, Georgia's decision to fund a "graduation coach" in every high school. The new full-time position is tasked with addressing dropout rates by working directly with

Table 6.1. Unrestricted Spending per Elementary School Pupil, California

Category	Low-poverty schools	High-poverty schools
Unrestricted	$4,409	$3,621
Compensatory education	23	454
Special education	687	603
Other categorical	376	730
Local restricted	142	112
Maintenance and operations	476	606
Total	$6,113	$6,126

Source: Rose et al. (2006).

the students at the highest risk of dropping out in each school (Jacobson 2008). While this strategy represents one distinct approach to addressing truancy, other approaches—such as small schools, magnet schools, and redesigned schools—rely on a different model, to which this kind of specialization represents interference. Similarly, in some districts, the local candidate pool does not uncover anyone with the appropriate skills or availability. Or some schools may not be battling a dropout problem and may instead need a different kind of assistance more appropriately tailored to the school's students. Further, in cases where the more disadvantaged students attend larger schools, this per school allocation makes a smaller per pupil investment in the needier students (since more students in the school share the one funded position).

For those wanting more innovation in education, increased state prescription on use of funds is a problem. The thinking is that new school models (not yet apparent to state policymakers) could enhance efficiency by either increasing results or decreasing costs. In this vein, state prescriptions for resource use serve as an obstacle to innovation, effectively locking in the current approach to schooling.

Also relevant, the evidence on the burdens of compliance with state prescriptions would also suggest that state-imposed decisions about resource allocation add to the educational bureaucracy that has long been identified as part of the problem.

Finally, proposals to centralize spending decisions to the state level conflict with existing accountability reforms. Simply put, states cannot hold districts and schools accountable for student performance when states decide resource use.

So again, while centralizing decisions about resource use to the state level solves some problems, it creates others. Like a wicked problem, the goals for America's education finance system will not be realized by simply tinkering with state prescriptions for resource use.

Devolve Decisions about Resource Use to the School or District

The counterproposal to centralizing decisions to states is to devolve decisions about resource use to schools (or even to districts). A quick scan of education news coverage points to a revival of interest in school-based decisionmaking. Districts in Chicago and New York have devolved authority to some schools, and what started as a pilot program for decentralizing authority in Boston has grown steadily. Houston also has decentralized some level of authority to all schools, and Colorado just passed a bill allowing schools to opt out of some labor agreements and other restrictions (Robelen 2008). At the time of writing, proposals in Connecticut, Massachusetts, and Nevada would enable more school-based resource decisions (Gewertz 2007). And to many, the growth of charter schools is another example of the movement toward freeing schools from central office rules and moving decisions down to the building level.

The logic behind devolving resource decisions to lower levels parallels the criticisms of the above proposal to centralize decisions. Namely, devolving authority to schools reflects the notion that school personnel are better equipped than district administrators to use their resources efficiently and effectively to meet student needs. As state and federal reforms move accountability for student performance to the school level, some policymakers have suggested that new accountability should be accompanied with more school-based authority. When building leaders are able to make decisions, the reasoning goes, those decisions can be tailored to the unique needs of their students, thereby resulting in more efficient, effective, and possibly innovative use of resources (Goertz and Stiefel 1998).[1]

While lumped together here, devolving decisions to districts and devolving decisions to schools are not necessarily the same proposal. Freeing up resources so districts can make decisions with little state interference can be intended to produce more coherent, more efficient spending. Yet, as has been extensively discussed in this book, many districts do not distribute the flexible resources they already have equitably or strategically across schools. As such, changing the state funding structure to devolve decisions to districts leaves intact other elements of the system that confound the basic intentions of the reform. Since much has already been made of these points, this section instead focuses on proposals to devolve decisions about resource use to schools.

For policymakers, several questions surface: If school leaders have more autonomy over resource decisions, will that make any difference in how schools use resources? When provided with greater spending autonomy, what choices do school leaders make? Do those choices differ meaningfully from current practice, and will students benefit from them?

With more efforts under way, some evidence is emerging that provides insights into this proposal's potential for change. Studies of early implementation of decentralization found that almost none of the early decentralization initiatives gave school-level leaders control over money and staff (Olson 1997; Stiefel et al. 2003). Clearly, an important factor of decentralization efforts is what gets decentralized. As one report suggests, decentralization hinges on devolving staff salaries, staff assignments, staff responsibilities, and selection of teachers (Bimber 1994).

While the range of examples on which to draw insights has grown, the catch in most policy examples is that they do not devolve all these different aspects of resource decisions. For instance, Goertz and Stiefel (1998), in their study of modest decentralization efforts in four districts (where schools were given freedom over staffing assignments purchased with some funds), find that building leaders used flexible resources in very traditional ways—reducing class size, expanding preschool, and purchasing professional development and materials for new curricula—and that no new innovations emerged. A U.S. General Accounting Office report (1994) on site-based management in three districts reports that school leaders chose to use their flexibility to add full-day kindergarten, extended-day programs, special education and gifted/talented programs, and new courses. Changes in budgeting included adjustments to spending on staff, supplies, and equipment. Another study finds that increasing the share of flexible resources resulted in structural changes, for example, offering reading programs within high schools (Carnoy, Elmore, and Siskin 2003).

Some might think the results sound promising or perhaps reassuring in the sense that schools do not appear to make matters worse by using their freedoms to make bad decisions. Then again, the results hardly suggest that granting partial autonomies, as was the case here, is a viable solution to the problems inherent in the larger finance structure described herein.

In a recent study of the Ohio school system, the CRPE team compared schools in centralized and decentralized districts with charter and private schools for evidence of how resources are used with fewer constraints. In addition, with some evidence that entrepreneurial principals can work the system to evade typical constraints, the team took nominations for entrepreneurial principals in order to look for such patterns in spending decisions. Table 6.2 depicts a typology of schools arrayed by the different types of autonomies afforded them.

The findings from this study indicate the following:

- Schools with more autonomies were able to make trade-offs so they could hire more teachers for their students. Further, schools with greater autonomies were more able to take advantage of these trade-offs than were schools with only limited autonomies.[2]

Table 6.2. School-Level Resource Autonomies Differ among School Types

School types	Key Areas of School-Level Resource Autonomy			
	Control over allocation of personnel to responsibilities	Control over allocation of resources across functional categories (e.g., pupil support, administration, etc.)	Control over number of teachers	Control over teacher compensation
Schools in centralized districts				
Schools in centralized districts with "entrepreneurial" principals	✓			
Schools in decentralized districts	✓	✓	✓	
Charter schools	✓	✓	✓	✓
Private schools	✓	✓	✓	✓

Source: Roza, Davis, and Guin (2007).

- While schools with entrepreneurial principals did garner more resources from their districts, they were not able to make trade-offs between staff positions.
- Schools with autonomy over teacher salary chose to hire more teacher FTEs at lower overall salaries. For example, one private school principal in the dataset described her school staffing in the following way:

> We have a very confusing schedule, but it fits our needs and allows us to get the most from our staff. Most of the K–8 grades have one full-time teacher each. The 4th grade teacher does two periods of counseling a day. These two periods are covered by the ESL and Spanish teacher. Fifth grade is split between two full-time staff members, but each spends half time as the grade-level teacher. The other half of their time is spent as a half-time librarian and computer education instructor (respectively). Seventh grade is covered by a teacher part of the day; the other part of her day is spent teaching physical

education to all grades. When this teacher is teaching P.E., the 7th grade class is covered by a part-time teacher. This part-time teacher teaches three classes/day of social studies and then she teaches music (two periods/week) and art for three periods/week. There is another part-time music teacher who comes in two days/week.

Box 6.1 incorporates these findings with the research literature to demonstrate how findings from this study could be used to predict the relationship between different levels of school-based autonomy over resources and allocation patterns. Of particular relevance is the tendency to try to employ more teachers per pupil and the trade-offs that schools with teacher salary freedoms make between salary and FTEs. Restrictions on teacher salaries, then, serve as a formidable barrier to some resource allocation changes that schools might pursue. Schools in decentralized districts typically lack freedom over salaries, which certainly constrains the scope of their other freedoms.[3]

Similar results have been found in studies of schools in England and Wales (Levačić 1995). Where schools were granted significant resource autonomies, including freedom over teacher hiring, schools did appear to make more tailored and more efficient decisions about resource use. While schools were required to follow teacher compensation schedules, they were also able to use funds saved on lower-salaried teachers for other purposes (including other staff). Interestingly, schools did not do as some had feared

---

Box 6.1. Types of Autonomy and Resource Allocation Patterns

Minimal constraints on	*were associated with*
Allocation of personnel to responsibilities	Smaller increments of staff (partial FTEs); however, this is difficult to determine with available data
Allocation of resources across functional categories (e.g., pupil support, administration, etc.)	More classroom teachers at the expense of specialists
Number of teachers	More teachers, as is fiscally feasible (constraints on salaries will prevent the school from making trade-offs between salary and FTEs)
Teacher compensation	Lower, more differentiated salaries

and hire only junior teachers to save funds. Rather, schools in the Barsetshire study indicated that they wanted pay for the best candidates, and they followed through on that intention when their budgets allowed.

With the flexibility of local management, schools were able to hire more part-time teachers to fill resource gaps from year to year. This allowed for an easier adjustment to fluctuations in need. Reports by Her Majesty's Inspectorate (1992) and Maychell (1994) show an increase in temporary contracts in locally managed schools. It seems that local management may have sparked a dual labor market in which most teachers are permanent employees but some are hired part time or temporarily to provide flexibility.

What, then, would happen if individual schools were freed from existing constraints on resource allocation? Clearly, the data indicate that schools with fewer constraints can and often do use their funds in different, more efficient-looking ways. That said, the differences are greatly muted when only some of the constraints are lifted. Where schools do not have freedom over teacher salaries or teacher hiring, they are not able to make the same trade-offs. In most decentralization proposals, critical autonomies are left off the table, and thus changes are made by tinkering with portions of decisions.

But in the context of creating a highly functioning education finance system, even promising models of decentralization fall short. By itself, decentralization cannot work: it only targets one aspect of the finance system. Success will depend in large part on other critical policy components. First, proposals about decentralizing spending decisions will not mesh with accountability reforms unless schools are funded equitably within districts. Funds must still be channeled from the state through districts to schools, and many decentralization proposals fall short on the details of how that would work. The most advanced proposal is summarized in a Thomas B. Fordham Institute publication, *Fund the Child* (2006). In this decentralization model, funds are driven out via weighted student formulas from states to districts and then to schools. The proposal then assumes states and districts dramatically change the roles they have traditionally played to honor school-based decisions about resource use.

A second critical component is one proving particularly hard for districts to consider in the context of other existing aspects of the finance model: granting schools flexibility over hiring and salaries. Without such autonomies, schools will not be able to better link their expenditures with the real value of what is provided to students.

It is a wicked problem, and the goals for America's education finance system will not be realized only by changing the locus of control.

Create Accountability: Define Desired Outcomes and Impose Consequences

No Child Left Behind and state accountability policies are part of what some had hoped would force an overhaul in the system that would drive resources to be used with increased effectiveness. In theory, at least, the idea has been to move away from a compliance model based on categorical program support to an accountability model (Cross and Roza 2007). By holding districts accountable for student performance (as measured at the school level), the reform suggests that districts (and perhaps schools) hold the key to unlocking student performance. In other words, these accountability reforms imply a belief that if staff in districts and schools do their jobs correctly, student performance will increase. The accountability clauses, it follows, are the motivation. Rather than directly tackle the money, this solution seeks to redefine roles, responsibilities, and relations within the system of public education.

Here, again, changing accountability alone cannot fix a wicked problem. First and foremost, accountability reforms that do not come with changes in how decisions about resource use are made create inconsistencies for the reform. Specifically, schools and districts wonder how the public can hold districts and schools accountable for student performance if decisions about resource use are made at the state, rather than the district, level. On the face of it, accountability reforms in some ways conflict with state policies to prescribe resource use.

The problem, in part, is that accountability reforms are set in motion by one group of policymakers and not completely embraced by all those with decisionmaking powers throughout the system. As an example, consider one state official tasked with implementing a state program to boost performance in low-performing districts and schools. When asked who in the system should be accountable for how the resources were used, the state official replied: "Well, I guess we all are. We're all part of the decision. The feds, the state department, the district, and the student." Unfortunately, her view does not align with the accountability structures put in place by state and federal reforms.

The comment touches on a key problem. In a system where decisions about resource use are so muddled, with no one locus of control, one must question whether the notion of accountability can be applied in ways that leverage any of the intended changes.

Here again, while accountability might be the right solution for part of the problem, without addressing the other dimensions of the problem, its effect is negated.

Finding Solutions to Wicked Problems

According to Jeff Conklin's definition of wicked problems, Americans are not likely to fully understand the problem of education finance until they have come up with a viable solution. Because none of the solutions that have been implemented thus far has been successful, Americans have not yet reached a complete understanding of what they are dealing with. And since they can't comprehend the extent of it, it is difficult to address the problem. How is it possible to break free from this bind?

It seems that a problem as complex as school finance reform may require an equally complicated solution—one that addresses the inter-relationships between stakeholders at different levels and clarifies roles for a more coherent, efficient, and equitable system. Each idea discussed here is not useless, but by itself, each proposed remedy cannot fix the system and will not have its intended effect. Only a multidimensional effort will be able to bring about a more effective solution.

7

A Multidimensional Solution
Elements of a Coherent, Aligned, Efficient Education Finance System

The point of six chapters detailing such incoherent spending patterns is not to attach blame or to cite specific areas for improvement in the current system. Rather, it is to demonstrate from the school vantage point just how and why the different parts of the system sever the link between spending and student outcomes. The hope is that these data provide the context for understanding how badly the current finance system is failing. The education finance system at hand is not working, and no single, simple policy lever can convert it into a high-performing finance system. The problems involve different levels of government and a multitude of actors in the system. The processes for allocating funds from one level to the next are fraught with unintended consequences, so school distribution and use of funds lacks any plausible connection to student learning. Few in the system understand how the money is used, since the system lacks any real transparency. And proposed strategies to overhaul the system cannot work, as each serves to modify only one dimension of a multidimensional problem.

The country is also facing a new challenge brought on by an economic recession and forecasts of budget tightening in nearly all public-service sectors. Improved results for students are unlikely to come from large new investments in public education. Rather, the system can only improve if it learns to do more with less. In this environment, amid the current spending patterns, changing the system is a national imperative.

Rather than specify remedies intended to alleviate different symptoms of the disease, this chapter takes a different approach. It starts from scratch, redefining the purpose of an education finance system and its desired attributes, and from there proposes design elements needed to build a system that meets those specifications.

Core Purpose and Desired Attributes of a Redesigned Finance System

The paramount purpose of an education finance system is to channel and deliver public funds to be used for educating students. This core function is so obvious that it goes underappreciated. Yet it is anything but trivial. The public education finance system must be able to deploy funds from their originating source to those responsible for providing services.

Notice that the purpose of the finance system is not to specify how resources are used for educating students, which may be a surprise to some. Rather, a high-performing finance system is one where funds are deployed in ways that *induce* the best decisions about resource use, not necessarily one that dictates those decisions.

This assertion deserves some explanation. Decisions about resource use define the production process. Clearly, if the best decisions for resource use are known and clear to all, and consistent across different settings, then yes, the best decisions about resource use could be prescribed by the finance system. However, as it stands, neither of these conditions is currently met. Education research is extremely uncertain about what works best in any situation. And, in each state, complex and dynamic student populations exist in dramatically different settings that seem to interact with any given decision about resource use to produce entirely different outcomes for students. These two realities suggest that it makes the most sense for the finance system to in fact *not* prescribe uniform decisions about resource use. As will be clarified below, a well-functioning finance system tolerates different decisions about how to apply resources, but also provides the right incentives and conditions to prompt the best decisions about resource use.

For this exercise, this core purpose is mapped against a set of five desired attributes of a well-functioning finance model (figure 7.1). The desired attributes are the qualities of the system, not a description of how it is designed or how it works.

Figure 7.1. Designing a High-Performing School Finance System

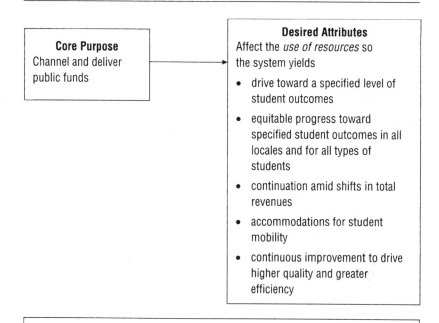

The first attribute addresses the system product—student outcomes—by directly acknowledging that a finance system must be driven by some specified outcomes for all students. In a system where the student outcomes are not yet at the level specified, the level serves as the target. The specified level of outcomes must exist for all students in all locales.

The second attribute follows from the first. That is, the finance system must ensure that student outcomes are sought equitably in all locales and for all types of students. Clearly, this is an important point because of the challenges posed by the differing conditions in cities, rural areas, or suburbs, and by the differing needs of various student types. For instance, the supply of quality labor can be a big challenge in some cities, while transportation costs can be a burden in rural areas. Similarly, poor and immigrant students pose different challenges than do others. In other words, the finance system is unbalanced (and inequitable) if it persistently yields substantially substandard outcomes for one group of students, while other groups are readily able to meet the specified outcomes. Where challenges are greater, the system will undoubtedly need to direct more funds. This is not to say that the services provided need to be the same in all areas or for all students, rather that funds are provided in ways that drive equitable progress toward specified outcomes for all students.

Third, a more commonly overlooked outcome is that a public education finance system ought to be able to weather fluctuations in revenues. As public taxing literature would indicate, while there are more and less stable revenue sources (for instance, property taxes are more stable than incomes taxes), all taxing policies are the product of inherently unpredictable public bodies. In addition, public education competes for revenues with other public priorities. As a consequence, the system cannot depend on a completely predictable, stable revenue source. Rather, the system ought to be able to deploy funds amid some fluctuation in the total pie. In other words, the mechanism by which funds are deployed must remain intact even when revenues increase or decrease.

Next, the system must allow for student mobility. Students do move. And, entire neighborhoods see enrollment patterns that accompany economic changes, demographic shifts, and even unforeseen natural disasters. Clearly, the finance system must be able to deliver funds that allow for student mobility.

The last desired attribute is that the finance system ought to foster excellence and efficiency. That means that the system should be designed to drive more effective and efficient uses of resources toward higher-quality services for students. Rather than determining how to use resources today, a highly functioning finance system would promote continuous improvement by adapting the best insights about high-quality and efficient services and discontinuing investments in efforts that do not yield the desired results.

Design Elements to Yield Desired Attributes

While the desired attributes describe what the system should be able to do, they do not specify how. The following seven design specifications describe how the system would be assembled to achieve the desired attributes.

1. Standards

Defining standards for student performance is how the system defines the "product" to be purchased with the funds. So for the finance system to work well, setting standards must be an integral part of the system. The standards need not be static; they can and should evolve over time to adapt with changes in national or state priorities and economic and labor needs. The system ought to be able to modify the desired outcomes for students and expect that the education system could accommodate that change.

2. Pupil-Based Formula to Allocate Dollars

To achieve its core purpose, the system must use some mechanism (a decision criterion or formula of some sort) that divides the funds out among the many providers—effectively determining how much money each receives. As pointed out in the desired attributes, the decision criteria should work amid shifts in tax revenues and shifts in providers. It should allow for student mobility, changes in student needs, and different local conditions. What is needed, then, is a pupil-based formula that allocates dollars (not purchased resources) based on pupils.

Note that the system currency ought to be dollars, not purchased resources (such as staff FTEs, services, professional development, and so on). In a system promoting continuous learning about the best decisions on resource use, the system cannot close down options by dictating how some funds are converted into purchased resources. And, as better options exist for how to apply funds to serve students, the funds must remain portable in the sense that programs can be eliminated and the funds moved to the better options. Remember that the job of the finance system is to disburse funds in ways that promote the best decisions about resource use, not to decide how to convert funds into purchased items.

3. Weighted Allocations for Different Student Types

Different students may pose different challenges. The finance system should accommodate these differences by differentiating allocations based on student needs. By weighting the pupil-based system based on student need, the finance system can take into account student types and geographic conditions and drive funds proportionately. It is in this way that the allocation formula can be modified to affect the supply of providers for all student types in all locales.

4. An Accountability System That Seeks the Most Effective Use of Funds

In order for the finance system to promote continuous improvement and greater efficiency, providers must innovate, test out new approaches, discard those that work poorly, and adopt improved practices when they emerge. In other words, continuous improvement actually requires that services not be uniform in their approach. To this end, the system needs a mechanism that promotes adapting the best insights about high-quality and efficient services, and at the same time discontinues investments in efforts that do not yield the desired results. For lack of a better word, this function is called *accountability*.

Unfortunately, "accountability" in today's education finance model has come to refer to an abstract notion with few practical results for different actors in the education system. Many think of it as a punitive term, forcing providers to shape up or suffer some consequences. Yet, in this model, accountability also has important implications for both providers and funders.

In the accountability model posed here, a clear distinction exists between funders and providers. Funders (those controlling how and where funds are disbursed) take on the role of investing funds across providers, continuously selecting providers who are most effective at providing services to students. In order to perform this function, funders must allow the providers to make consequential decisions so results can be attributed to the effect of the provider, and then move funds if and when one provider's outcomes are substandard and there is a more promising provider. In other words, accountability means that investments constantly seek higher quality. When there are no quality providers, the funder may realize that the funds offered are insufficient and the problem is with the supply. In this case, more funds may be needed to purchase the desired services in a particular locale or with a particular type of student.

Providers, too, have distinct roles. Providers must be free to use funds in ways they believe will most effectively produce the desired results for students, and they must be subject to another party's (the funder's) decisions about whether the results obtained are satisfactory. Herein lies the importance of the distinction between the two groups. The party allocating funds must not be the party determining the use of funds because if one party plays both these roles, it has neither the perspective nor the incentive to call its own efforts unsatisfactory or to look for alternatives.

This design element is a significant departure from the current relationship between states and district boards or between boards and schools. If we think of states as a funder of school boards, who are providers, then it is imperative that states do not decide how funds are used. Rather, school boards are held accountable for student outcomes. Both states and school boards need to know about best practices, and school boards must be willing to constantly change their practices to seek the best outcomes for students. If and when the results for students are unsatisfactory, the states must move funds from the school boards to other providers (possible reassigning schools to different school boards or other providers).

If we take the funder/provider relationship and apply it to school boards and schools (where school boards are the funders and schools are the providers), then the same consequences can exist. The relationship can work similarly if the school board funds schools, schools decide how funds are used, and both seek information about the best practices. Here again, if and when some schools yield substandard results, the board must withdraw funds from those schools and apply them to more effective schools.

It is true that accountability may feel like a punitive term in the sense that if services provided are substandard and other promising providers exist, funds will be moved away from substandard providers. It is precisely this relationship that creates the right incentives for continuous improvement toward desired outcomes.

But if the system is to promote higher-quality services, funding simply must be contingent on effectiveness. That is not to say that the problem may be insufficient funding. If providers yield substandard outcomes, and there are no other promising providers, the funding may be insufficient in the particular market (or with particular student needs) to fuel effective services.

5. Open Market for Providers

It follows, of course, that the system must be open to new providers. Many problems in current accountability schemes stem from the notion that with a single provider (via a single school or single school district), there are not alternative providers. As such, the system cannot move funds to more promising investments, and the systems are not aligned to push for continuous improvement.

6. Alignment of Functions and Clarity of Roles

The problem isn't that our current system doesn't recognize that the finance system must control the flow of dollars, set standards, and use some sort of accountability functions as key ingredients in the education system. Rather, much of the problem is that decisionmakers haven't recognized their role in the workings of finance, and thus haven't properly mixed in each ingredient.

These different dimensions need to be carefully integrated in order for them to work in concert and perform their desired functions. More specifically, in a financial transaction, those disbursing the funds are the ones purchasing the services. Those setting the standards are defining the product (what is purchased are the desired student outcomes). And accountability is what promotes higher-quality services and what prevents repeated investments in services that yield substandard outcomes.

Decisions about resource use define the production process and are therefore the object that these three functions are intended to influence. While stated before, this point bears restating. Disbursing funds, setting standards, and creating accountability are functions intended to influence how money is converted into purchased resources (through hires, creation of programs, and so on) toward creating student outcomes. While student outcomes are the end goal, students won't suddenly understand algebra better because the finance system has an accountability feature. Rather, the accountability feature, if it works, should influence decisions about who is hired to teach, what training he or she receives, and what other purchased resources (programs or services) are brought to bear on the student. It follows that accountability functions, and, similarly, funds distribution and standards setting, are designed to influence decisions about resource use. Decisions about resource use are the object of these functions.

As described as part of the accountability relationship, the system hinges on how all these the different functions are aligned. If the disbursing, standards setting, and accountability functions are to influence decisions about resource use, then decisions about resource use must take place at a different level of the system than at the locus of standard setting or accountability setting. In other words, those doling out the funds, defining the standards, and imposing accountability can't be the ones making decisions about resource use. Figure 7.2 summarizes the proposed assignment of tasks.

A critical component for alignment to work is clarity of roles. Funders must understand that they are funders, and not think and act like they are providers. Similarly, those making decisions about resource use should not raise funds, set standards, or hold themselves accountable.[1]

The implications for this kind of alignment of functions in today's education governance system are complicated. Our current system has many more than two levels. The funders, as described here, could be the federal, state, or local districts. And yet, all these governmental agencies also play a hand in controlling how resources are used. Take for instance the state role in the finance system, where states dole out funds, set standards, and help define accountability. Yet, states also prescribe decisions

Figure 7.2. Alignment of Key Tasks

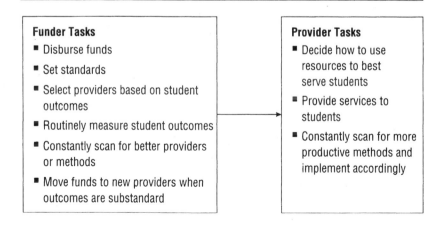

Funder Tasks
- Disburse funds
- Set standards
- Select providers based on student outcomes
- Routinely measure student outcomes
- Constantly scan for better providers or methods
- Move funds to new providers when outcomes are substandard

Provider Tasks
- Decide how to use resources to best serve students
- Provide services to students
- Constantly scan for more productive methods and implement accordingly

about resource use. The contradiction was described earlier: making decisions about how resources are used interferes with other key functions, including accountability.

7. Transparency in Student Outcomes and Most Productive Practices

If funders are to select providers effectively, they must do so based on constant and reliable evidence about student outcomes. Further, for providers to be highly productive—that is, produce the highest outcomes for the price—they need to constantly scan accurate data on effective practices and cost efficiency.

The result is the last design element, which suggests that a well-functioning finance system hinges upon the collection of reliable fiscal and student performance data. More specifically, transparency in results and use of funds needs to demonstrate the following:

- the performance of students served by different providers (by student type and locale),
- the effectiveness of new approaches to delivering services,
- what providers' decisions about resource use lead to more effective services, and
- the costs of different service options and how they might be optimized.

The transparent data are intended to inform funders, but also to fuel continuous improvement through innovation and adaptation.

Conclusion

Some might find this list of design elements a frustrating approach to reforming the school finance system, as it does not provide step-by-step instructions on how to get from the system in place to the system described here. And it is true, the governmental agencies in place today bear little resemblance to the "funders" and the "providers" outlined above. That said, as the last chapter demonstrated, solutions to wicked problems fail when the solution is crafted from the very flawed structures that serve as the basis of the current model.

So this chapter has approached the task of designing a high-functioning finance system with total disregard to the existing parts of the system. While trying to overlay the proposed aligned relationships on the current system is tricky, recognizing the need to redefine roles can help practical solutions emerge. Take for instance, the need to separate the functions of allocating resources, setting standards, and defining accountability from the function of making decisions about resource use. If states could recognize that they play some role in the first three, they might be convinced that they should not also take on the fourth.

While the road map to change is not a clear one, the endpoint can be defined. If public education is to accomplish goals that have never been met before, educators must search for new ideas, try out new models of teaching and learning, and always be ready to abandon a less productive practice in favor of a more effective one. A finance system based on these design specs can achieve these objectives.

In the immediate future, policymakers must recognize their hand in the current ineffective finance model. Further, they must seek progress toward a more highly functioning model, not by imposing new constraints but by figuring out what their role should be in a redesigned system.

Much work needs to be done, both in creating a road map and redefining roles. To attempt a lasting solution to the wicked problem of school finance, virtually all players in the system must be engaged in a coordinated and aligned solution for the benefit of our students.

Notes

Chapter 1. Fuzzy Math

1. Marguerite Roza, "Policy Inadvertently Robs Poor Schools to Benefit the Rich," *Seattle Post Intelligencer*, September 24, 2000.

2. Dallas was under a court order to spend desegregation money only on schools with a high percentage of minorities.

Chapter 2. Who's in Charge Here?

1. *Serrano v. Priest*, 5 Cal.3d 584 (1971) (Serrano I).

2. *San Antonio Independent School Dist. v. Rodriguez*, 411 U.S. 1 (1973).

3. See "The Catalog of Federal Domestic Assistance," http://www.cfda.gov (accessed October 29, 2008).

4. U.S. Department of Education, "Fund for the Improvement of Education–Programs of National Significance: 2005 Directed Grants," http://www.ed.gov/programs/fie/2005fie-directed.html (last modified August 30, 2006).

5. After adjusting for inflation, per pupil spending today is roughly double what it was 30 years ago. Yet, many analysts suggest that on average schools are producing only slightly better results than at earlier times. To be sure, the schools have absorbed a rising tide of children who have greater needs—more impoverished, more from single-parent families, more recent immigrants from countries where English is not their first language, and more with learning disabilities. But to some policymakers, education is literally becoming less productive.

Chapter 3. When Agendas Collide

1. These cost estimates are based on the latest available average levels of per pupil spending and teacher compensation in larger urban districts. The cost of employee benefits like health care and retirement benefits is estimated by looking at the cost differences between typical teacher benefits and the benefits enjoyed by the average worker in the private sector. Estimates for policies like class size reduction and hiring of teacher's aides also are conservative, attributing only a fraction of the likely total cost of the policies to contract provisions. For teacher professional development, only costs associated with mandatory additional days of paid training are included.

2. Districts would certainly need to keep commitments made to existing teachers, so new plans might apply only to new hires or to current teachers that chose to opt in.

3. Another indication that school administrators bear responsibility for many unquestioned expenditures is the fact that many policies and practices mandated by collective-bargaining contracts also exist in states and school districts where teachers do not have collective-bargaining rights.

Chapter 4. Driving Blind

1. Based on CRPE analysis of a large urban western district.

2. Unpublished findings by CRPE researchers.

3. At the time of writing, the one notable exception is in Oakland, California.

4. Comments provided by participants in "The Policymaker's Exchange 2000" at the Evans School of Public Affairs, University of Washington.

5. CRPE analysis of a midwestern urban district.

6. See, for instance, Rice (2000).

7. Information obtained via consulting arrangement with a large western school district.

Chapter 5. What Does It All Mean for Schools?

1. Analysis by CRPE researchers of Denver and Chicago finance data.

Chapter 6. A Wicked Problem: Why Typically Proposed Overhauls of the Finance System Are Guaranteed to Fail

1. Recent research on decentralization, accompanied by greater school control over resources, provides some evidence of a positive effect on student performance. A 1996 study of schools in Texas concluded that principals who carefully and steadily applied resources to interrelated organizational changes could bring about gains in achievement (Murnane and Levy 1996). A study of Chicago's decentralization effort in the 1990s

found that principals were able to inventively deploy resources in ways that appeared to boost achievement (Bryk, Camburn, and Louis 1999). A study of Boston's Pilot School Program found pilot students (in schools with greater authority over budget, curriculum, staffing, and governance) performed better than students in other Boston public schools (Tung, Ouimette, and Feldman 2004).

2. It should be noted that this study was not able to consider differences in teacher quality, which would be important in any full analysis of efficiency.

3. Also noteworthy are the minimal spending differences associated with entrepreneurial principals. While schools with entrepreneurial principals were described as ones that were doing things differently than other district schools, their staffing and expenditure data did not, in fact, greatly differ from public centralized schools.

Chapter 7. A Multidimensional Solution: Elements of a Coherent, Aligned, Efficient Education Finance System

1. The explanation for this line of thinking originates in classic economic and financial theory.

References

Bimber, Bruce A. 1994. *The Decentralization Mirage: Comparing Decisionmaking Arrangements in Four High Schools.* Santa Monica, CA: RAND Corporation.

Boston Consulting Group. 2007. "Cost Efficiency in Delaware Education." Jerry Gallagher, presentation, Education Finance Overview. Boston: Boston Consulting Group.

Bryk, Anthony S., Eric Camburn, and Karen S. Louis. 1999. "Professional Community in Chicago Elementary Schools: Facilitating Factors and Organizational Consequences." *Educational Administration Quarterly* 35(5): 751–81.

Carey, Kevin. 2002. *State Poverty-Based Education Funding: A Survey of Current Programs and Options for Improvement.* Washington, DC: Center on Budget and Policy Priorities.

Carnoy, Martin, Richard Elmore, and Leslie Santee Siskin, eds. 2003. *The New Accountability: High Schools and High-Stakes Testing.* New York: RoutledgeFalmer.

Celio, Mary Beth, and James Harvey. 2005. *Buried Treasure: Developing a Management Guide from Mountains of School Data.* Seattle: Center on Reinventing Public Education, University of Washington.

Chambers, Jay G. 1999. "Patterns of Variation in the Salaries of School Personnel: What Goes On Behind the Cost Index Numbers?" *Journal of Education Finance* 25(2): 255–80.

Coleman, James S., et al. 1966. *Equality of Educational Opportunity.* 2 vols. Washington, DC: U.S. Government Printing Office.

Conklin, Jeffrey. 2006. *Dialogue Mapping: Building Understanding of Wicked Problems.* Chichester: John Wiley & Sons.

Cooper, Paul. 1993. *Effective Schools for Disaffected Students.* London: Routledge.

Coopers & Lybrand, LLP. 1994. *Small Business Training and Preferences: A Report for VET Providers.* Sydney: New South Wales Department of Technical and Further Education (TAFE NSW).

Cross, Christopher T., and Marguerite Roza. 2007. "How the Federal Government Shapes and Distorts the Financing of K–12 Schools." School Finance Redesign Project Working Paper 1. Seattle: Center on Reinventing Public Education, University of Washington.

Duncombe, William, and John Yinger. 2004. "How Much More Does a Disadvantaged Student Cost?" Working Paper 60. Syracuse, NY: Center for Policy Research, Maxwell School of Syracuse University.

Education Trust–West, The. 2005. *California's Hidden Teacher Spending Gap: How State and District Spending Practices Shortchange Poor and Minority Students and Their Schools.* Oakland, CA: The Education Trust–West.

Fowler, William J., Jr. 2001. "Financial Reporting in the New Millennium." In *Education Finance in the New Millennium: AEFA 2001 Yearbook,* edited by Stephen Chaikind and William J. Fowler, Jr. (35–51). Larchmont, NY: Eye on Education.

Gewertz, Catherine. 2007. "Easing Rules over Schools Gains Favor." *Education Week* 26(28).

Goertz, Margaret E., and Leanna Stiefel. 1998. "School-Level Resource Allocation in Urban Public Schools." *Journal of Education Finance* 23:435–46.

Goldhaber, Dan, Michael DeArmond, and Scott DeBurgomaster. 2007. "Teacher Attitudes about Compensation Reform: Implications for Reform Implementation." School Finance Redesign Project Working Paper 20. Seattle: Center on Reinventing Public Education, University of Washington.

Griffith, Michael. 2008. "Education Funding: A National Perspective." PowerPoint presentation. Richmond: Virginia House of Delegates, House Appropriations Committee, Joint Subcommittee on K–12 Education Financing. http://hac.state.va.us/subcommittee/Joint_Sub_on_K-12_Education_Funding/08-18-08/School_Finance_Systems—08-18-08—color.pdf.

Guthrie, James W. 1996. "What Might Happen in American Education If It Were Known How Money Actually Is Spent?" In *Where Does the Money Go?,* edited by Lawrence O. Picus and James L. Wattenbarger (253–68). Thousand Oaks, CA: Corwin Press.

Hansen, Janet S., and Marguerite Roza. 2005. "Trying Decentralization for Real This Time." *Education Week* 24(44): 40, 52.

Hassel, Bryan, and Marguerite Roza. 2007. "Funding the Child: Getting Results in South Carolina through Weighted Student Funding." Columbia: The South Carolina Policy Council and the Thomas B. Fordham Institute.

Her Majesty's Inspectorate. 1992. *The Implementation of Local Management of Schools.* London: Her Majesty's Stationery Office.

Jacobson, Linda. 2008. "States Eye Looser Rein on Districts: More Operating Leeway Seen as Spurring Local Improvement." *Education Week* 27(26): 1, 18.

Jennings, John F. 2000. "Title I: Its Legislative History and Its Promise." *Phi Delta Kappan* 81(7): 516–22.

Joint Select Committee on Public School Finance. 2004. *Report to the Legislature.* Austin, TX: Joint Select Committee on Public School Finance.

Krop, Cathy S., Stephen J. Carroll, and Randy L. Ross. 1995. *Tracking K–12 Education Spending in California: Who, Where, and How Much?* Santa Monica, CA: Institute on Education & Training, RAND Corporation.

Lee, Robert D., Jr., Ronald W. Johnson, and Philip G. Joyce. 2004. *Public Budgeting Systems.* 7th ed. Sudbury, MA: Jones & Bartlett.

Levačić, Rosalind. 1995. *Local Management of Schools: Analysis and Practice.* Buckingham: Open University Press.

Loveless, Tom, Steve Farkas, and Ann Duffett. 2008. *High-Achieving Students in the Era of NCLB.* Washington, DC: Thomas B. Fordham Institute.

Marzano, Robert J. 2000. *A New Era of School Reform: Going Where the Research Takes Us.* Aurora, CO: Mid-Continent Research for Education and Learning.

Maychell, Karen. 1994. *Counting the Cost: The Impact of LMS on Schools' Patterns of Spending.* Slough: National Foundation for Education Research.

McClure, Phyllis P., and Ruby Martin. 1969. *Title I of ESEA: Is It Helping Poor Children?* Washington, DC: National Association for the Advancement of Colored People Legal Defense and Education Fund.

McNeil, Michele. 2007. "As Budgets Swell, Spending Choices Get New Scrutiny." *Education Week* 26(29).

Miller, Larry, Marguerite Roza, and Claudine Swartz. 2005. "A Cost Allocation Model for Shared District Resources: A Means for Comparing Spending across Schools." School Finance Redesign Project Working Paper 4. Seattle: Center on Reinventing Public Education, University of Washington.

Monk, David H., Christopher F. Roellke, and Brian O. Brent. 1996. *What Education Dollars Buy: An Examination of Resource Allocation Patterns in New York State Public School Systems.* New Brunswick, NJ: Consortium for Policy Research in Education.

Murnane, Richard, and Frank Levy. 1996. "Evidence from Fifteen Schools in Austin, Texas." In *Does Money Matter? The Effect of School Resources on Student Achievement and Adult Success,* edited by Gary Burtless (93–96). Washington, DC: Brookings Institution Press.

National Education Association. 2005. *Rankings and Estimates: Rankings of the States 2004 and Estimates of School Statistics 2005.* Washington, DC: National Education Association.

Nyhan, Ronald C., and Mohamad G. Alkadry. 1999. "The Impact of School Resources on Student Achievement Test Scores." *Journal of Education Finance* 25(2): 211–28.

Odden, Allan. 2007. "Redesigning School Finance Systems: Lessons from CRPE Research." Policy Brief 50. Philadelphia: Consortium for Policy Research in Education, University of Pennsylvania.

Odden, Allan, Sarah Archibald, Mark Ferminick, and Betheny Gross. 2003. "Defining School-Level Expenditure Structures That Reflect Educational Strategies." *Journal of Education Finance* 28(3): 323–56.

Olson, Lynn. 1997. "Shaking Things Up." *Education Week* 17(2): 29–31.

Petrides, Lisa, and Thad Nodine. 2005. "Online Development Education: Who's Ready?" *Community College Journal* 76(2).

Rice, Jennifer King. 2000. *Teacher Quality: Understanding the Effectiveness of Teacher Attributes.* Washington, DC: Economic Policy Institute.

Robelen, Erik. 2008. "Colorado Moves Ahead on Ambitious K–12 Package." *Education Week* 27(36).

Rose, Heather, Jon Sonstelie, and Ray Reinhard. 2006. *School Resources and Academic Standards in California: Lessons from the Schoolhouse.* San Francisco: Public Policy Institute of California.

Rothstein, Richard. 2004. *Class and Schools: Using Social, Economic, and Educational Reform to Close the Black-White Achievement Gap.* Washington, DC: Economic Policy Institute.

Roza, Marguerite. 2003. *Real Dollars for Real Teachers: The Case in Baltimore.* Baltimore: Advocates for Children and Youth, Inc.

———. 2005. "District Fiscal Practices and Their Effect on School Spending." Paper prepared for the Aspen Institute Congressional Program, *The Challenge of Education Reform: Standards, Accountability, Resources, and Policy.* Seattle: Center on Reinventing Public Education, University of Washington.

———. 2007a. *Allocation Anatomy: How District Policies That Deploy Resources Can Support (or Undermine) District Reform Strategies.* School Finance Redesign Project Working Paper 24. Seattle: Center on Reinventing Public Education, University of Washington.

———. 2007b. *Frozen Assets: Rethinking Teacher Contracts Could Free Billions for School Reform.* Washington, DC: Education Sector.

———. 2007c. "How Resource Allocation Strategies Result in Fiscal Instability amidst Enrollment Declines." Paper presented at the 32nd annual conference of the American Education Finance Association, Baltimore, March 23.

———. 2007d. "Equitable Distribution Policies and Practices: Implications for States and Districts." Presentation to the National Comprehensive Center for Teacher Quality Issue Forum, From Planning to Action: Implementation of the Highly Qualified Teacher Plans, Washington, D.C., March 28.

———. 2009. "Breaking Down School Budgets." *Education Next* 9(3).

Roza, Marguerite, and Paul T. Hill. 2004. "How Within-District Spending Inequities Help Some Schools to Fail." In *Brookings Papers on Education Policy: 2004,* edited by Diane Ravitch (201–28). Washington, DC: Brookings Institution Press.

———. 2006. "How Can Anyone Say What's Adequate if Nobody Knows How Money Is Spent?" In *Courting Failure,* edited by Eric Hanushek (235–56). Stanford, CA: Education Next Books.

Roza, Marguerite, Tricia Davis, and Kacey Guin. 2007. "Spending Choices and School Autonomy: Lessons from Ohio Elementary Schools." School Finance Redesign Project Working Paper 21. Seattle: Center on Reinventing Public Education, University of Washington.

Roza, Marguerite, Kacey Guin, and Tricia Davis. 2008. *What Is the Sum of the Parts? How Federal, State, and District Funding Streams Confound Efforts to Address Different Student Types.* Seattle: Center on Reinventing Public Education, University of Washington.

Roza, Marguerite, Larry Miller, and Paul Hill. 2005. *Strengthening Title I to Help High-Poverty Schools: How Title I Funds Fit into District Allocation Patterns.* Seattle: Center on Reinventing Public Education, University of Washington.

Roza, Marguerite, Kacey Guin, Betheny Gross, and Scott DeBurgomaster. 2007. "Do Districts Fund Schools Fairly?" *Education Next* 7(4): 68–73.

Stiefel, Leanna, Ross Rubenstein, and Robert Berne. 1998. "Intra-District Equity in Four Large Cities: Data, Methods, Results." *Journal of Education Finance* 23(4): 447–67.

Stiefel, Leanna, Amy Ellen Schwartz, Carole Portas, and Dae Yeop Kim. 2003. "School Budgeting and School Performance: The Impact of New York City's Performance Driven Budgeting Initiative." *Journal of Education Finance* 28(3): 403–24.

Thomas B. Fordham Institute. 2006. *Fund the Child: Tackling Inequity and Antiquity in School Finance.* Washington, DC: Thomas B. Fordham Institute.

Tung, Rosann, Monique Ouimette, and Jay Feldman. 2004. *How Are Boston Pilot School Students Faring? Student Demographics, Engagement, and Performance 1998–2003.* Boston: Center for Collaborative Education.

U.S. General Accounting Office. 1994. *Education Reform: School-Based Management Results in Changes in Instruction and Budgeting.* HEHS-94-135. Washington, DC: U.S. General Accounting Office.

West, Martin R., and Paul E. Peterson. 2007. *School Money Trials: The Legal Pursuit of Educational Adequacy.* Washington, DC: Brookings Institution Press.

Winans, Dave. 2005. "The Bill's Come Due." *NEA Today* 24(2): 24–29.

Wildavsky, Aaron, and Naomi Caiden. 2004. *The New Politics of the Budgetary Process.* 5th ed. New York: Longman.

About the Author

Marguerite Roza is a research associate professor at the University of Washington's College of Education and a senior scholar at the Center on Reinventing Public Education. For over a decade, her research has focused on education spending and productivity, digging deep into education spending records to follow resources as they are deployed across schools, classrooms, and students. Much of her work traces spending patterns back to the various policy decisions that prompted them. Her analyses of fiscal policies and their implications for resources at school and classroom levels have prompted changes in education finance policy at all levels in the education system. She has written more than 40 articles and monographs in a wide variety of publications. Currently she serves as a nonresident senior fellow at the Brookings Institution, at Education Sector, and at the Rockefeller Institute.

Marguerite Roza earned her Ph.D. in education from the University of Washington. Prior to that, she served as a lieutenant in the U.S. Navy, teaching thermodynamics at the Naval Nuclear Power School. She has a B.S. from Duke University and has studied at the London School of Economics and the University of Amsterdam. She lives in Seattle with her husband, Scott Roza, and their four daughters.

Index